Nutro's Story
of Pioneering Among Giants

Billion Dollar Kibble

CHRISTIE COOPER
& MARY HOOKS

Billion Dollar Kibble
Nutro's Story of Pioneering Among Giants

Softcover ISBN: 979-8-9949231-0-8
eBook ISBN: 979-8-9949231-1-5

For more information, visit CooperConsultingGroup.com

Printed in the United States of America

Contents

Foreword 9

Introduction 11

1 Paw Prints on My Heart 13

2 The Genesis: From the U.K. to the USA 17

3 Building the Empire 31

4 The Lineage: From Mustang to Milky Way 37

5 A Leap of Faith 49

6 Trees Don't Grow to the Sky 53

7 Belly-to-Belly Strategy #1: Differential 57

8 Belly-to-Belly Strategy #2: Conversion 61

9 Belly-to-Belly Strategy #3: Recommendation Is King 65

10 Belly-to-Belly Strategy #4: People 69

11 Creating Camelot: The Nutro Culture 77

12 Catalysts to Success: The Product 95

13 Catalysts to Success: Taking a New Initiative 99

14 Catalysts to Success: Taking a Big Plunge 105

15 Lessons Learned: Dedicated to Entrepreneurs 111

16 Memories 117

Author's Note 123

Appendix 131

Acknowledgments 133

About the Authors 143

To the many outstanding people who have contributed to the growth of Nutro. Their names are listed in the acknowledgments.

Foreword

We learn from each encounter we have throughout our lives. At the age of 50, I took a leap of faith that would later become one of the proudest moments in my life.

This leap of faith happened during the 1970s. I was an outside sales representative working for a distributor of hard good pet supplies called Lee Mar. I knew *of* John Saleen, as he was the then-owner of Nutro. I intentionally sat by him at lunch while attending the World Wide Pet Show Association in the mid-70s. The conversation I ended up having with him would change the trajectory of my life.

As I look back over the years, I realize that my colleagues and I didn't do anything very complicated; we just successfully developed an entrée that was hard to say no to. We listened to what the consumer wanted and created a need in their mind that our product would solve their pets' problems. I can't recall a store that we did not get our products into.

This is the amazing story of how a company that was purchased for $300,000 in 1976 went on to be sold for *$2 billion* in 2009—and the people who helped make that happen. I am excited to be a part of this book's journey, having Christie Cooper and my daughter, Mary Hooks, author the story and for all of us who were a part of this amazing story.

Good selling, Tiger!

—Ed Brown

Introduction

The company formerly known as the *Nutro Dog Food Company*, our employer for 20 years, had been privately held and independently owned since 1931. A man named Herben Serois founded this obscure, humble, remarkable business to create a type of health food for dogs. By formulating a product with qualities vastly different from their competitors, Nutro has become a true icon in the pet industry.

"Selling one bag at a time" was an expression that members of the organization fondly used to express the great lengths to which individual salespeople would go to promote Nutro products. Ultimately, these products created a movement within the pet industry. The company's competitors considered its associates to be almost cult-like in their faith toward this approach. In fact, these employees believed so much in what they were selling that there was no other option for anyone except to feed their pets the "World's Best Dog Food." And these are the very people who have helped us write this book.

When we set out to write this book, we were overwhelmed by the warm reception and encouragement we received from our colleagues. From the first planning meeting to contacting John Saleen's children—Steve Saleen, founder of Saleen Mustangs; Mike Saleen, retired Deputy District Attorney; and Robyn Saleen, college professor—and then speaking to our Nutro family members, we realized that the timing could not have been more perfect.

People told us, "I'm delighted to hear that somebody has picked that up as a project to record," and "I thought about doing that 10 times myself, just never had the time," and "Yes, I am happy to participate!" Some told us it felt like a good therapy session to reminiscence about past stories. This process has given us the wonderful opportunity to connect with the colleagues we think of as family, many of whom we'd not spoken to in years. We wanted each person to share their favorite stories and their view on what made the culture so special and what drove Nutro into the hearts and minds of our loyal pet parents.

This book aims to give other entrepreneurs the inspiration to achieve success and greatness. It will also share the strategies and cultural insights that allowed a solopreneur to launch a company into the hearts and minds of millions of consumers.

1

Paw Prints On My Heart

"If there are no dogs in Heaven, then when I die I want to go where they went."
—*Will Rogers*

There was a bleak and ominous weather forecast that day in Cheyenne, Wyoming, the type of day that would keep most people indoors and attached to their woodburning stoves to ward off the dampness and chill. But there was no way the young newlyweds from California were going to stay home. Howard and Christie were high school sweethearts and were married as young adults—really, still teenagers. After Howard graduated high school, he spent a semester at the local community college. However, he felt this experience was not going to get him to his ultimate goal of being a Los Angeles deputy sheriff, so he joined the Air Force. After graduating basic training, he found himself stationed in Cheyenne. Shortly after, he married Christie. Instead of sunny days and great weather in Southern California, they were about to set off to Bushnell, Nebraska, in hopes of selecting their newest family member.

While exiting Interstate 80, the already dark skies seemed to grow black. The young couple had chosen to watch *Children of the Corn* the previous evening, and they suddenly felt as though the movie was coming to life. The cryptic directions they received took them through a small town surrounded by fields of corn so tall and lush they seemed impenetrable. After driving through the tranquil community without seeing a soul, the directions took them to the front gates of a cemetery at the edge of town. The dirt-lined road curved up toward a rustic barn at the top of a hill.

"Hey Babe, do you think we should really be going this direction?" Christie asked with a lump in her throat.

Howard, eager to get to their destination, replied, "Quit worrying! And stop thinking about the movie you just watched. Everything will be fine."

With their hearts in their throat and dark clouds overhead, they continued on their trek.

They rationalized it was Sunday, and perhaps most townspeople were church-goers and were still worshipping. Howard placed their truck in gear and slowly ascended the hill. As they neared the end of the cemetery, Christie pointed to the silhouette of a large dog. Highlighted by the morning sun, a black Labrador with a masculine jawline and broad chest sat rock steady as it watched them approach. Barking loudly, the dog alerted the farmhouse residents of the approaching strangers. Moments later, two young children appeared behind the black Lab. The couple finally breathed a sigh of relief as they eagerly got out of their truck to find 15 black and yellow, somewhat pudgy puppies scampering around with the two children. Howard and Christie were happily mauled by 15 possible new family members.

Howard fell in love with a Dijon mustard-colored female Labrador. At 7 weeks old, she had one more week before she could accompany them home to their apartment. Christie waited anxiously for their "baby" to come home, and once she arrived, they settled on the name Buffy. They took Buffy everywhere with them; as far as they were concerned, Buffy was not just a dog. She was truly the couple's first child before they started their human family.

Several years later, the couple moved back to California and expanded their family with the birth of their daughter. Buffy was mesmerized by this new infant to whom everyone was paying so much attention. Sniffing and licking the baby quickly became commonplace. By the time the couple's daughter began to walk, Buffy was the perfect training aid for standing and walking. Buffy was always compliant, even with an occasional ear or tail tug as their child struggled to maintain her wobbly stance.

Howard and Christie, now approaching 30, awoke one morning to realize Buffy did not seem quite right. Her enthusiastic morning kiss and snuggle went missing as she lay on her bed. The couple, fraught with concern, called in sick to work and took Buffy to the local vet. The vet gave a thorough examination and concluded that Buffy needed an ultrasound on her abdomen, which he was not equipped to conduct. Christie did some quick research as to who in Southern California was the best canine internal medicine specialist and found a medical group in Santa Monica that they contacted at once.

A very empathetic receptionist greeted the couple and took down the necessary information. The staff set up an examining room with the latest technology, ready to receive Buffy. While examining her, the vet told the couple, "Buddy, my black Lab, loved to duck hunt until his arthritis kept him out of the field. I was lucky to have him till he was 15." His story comforted the couple and gave them confidence that he would provide the best care and compassion while trying to save their beloved family member.

The vet went on to say how stoic dogs can be. Even in Buffy's final moments, she never complained; she simply continued to thump her tail happily as she lay on the examination table. There was no limit that day to the amount of money the couple would have spent to save her. Buffy was their first family member, and they remember her fondly, referring to Buffy as the world's best dog.

Most people can easily recall the time they brought a new pet into their household, the time their pet found them, or even the difficult end of life decisions that some people are forced to make. Whether the event is joyous or sobering, one thing remains the same: ***pets are our family***. We bestow upon them human traits and emotions. We treat our dogs and cats as if they are our children. People are spending at an all-time high on their pets, especially in pet foods.

And that's where our part of the story begins.

2

The Genesis: From the U.K. to the USA

*"Do not follow where the path may lead.
Go instead where there is no
path and leave a trail."*
—Ralph Waldo Emerson

FIGURE 1: PHOTO OF JAMES SPRATT, UNKNOWN YEAR

With thanks to the American Kennel Club Archives Library.

Let's travel back in time to just after the turn of the 19th century. Shipping had become the lifeblood of the world's economy, connecting manufacturers to customers and allowing the exchange of goods cross-continentally. It was on one such transatlantic trip around the year 1850 that James Spratt (Figure 1), an American inventor and entrepreneur, set sail from the United States for England.

An electrician by trade and an Englishman of seemingly endless ingenuity, Spratt earned numerous patents for his efforts in

Hermetic Sealing, Lightning Conductors, Innovation in Cattle Feeding, and Meat-Fibrine Dog Cakes. The last of these revolutionized the way that people all over the globe fed their dogs. The product shown in Figure 2 was Spratt's foray into commercially prepared pet food.

FIGURE 2: SPRATT'S FIBRINE DOG CAKES ADVERTISEMENT

With thanks to the British Newspaper Archive (www.BritishNewspaperArchive.co.uk).

James Spratt's love for dogs compelled him to seek a way to elevate the way that people fed dogs. It was Spratt's belief that "[the] food makes the dog."[1]

While at a boatyard in Liverpool, England, he observed stray dogs being thrown scraps and hard biscuits left over from the sailor's rations. These biscuits, known as hardtack,[2] were made of flour, salt, and water. They were briefly baked and then left to harden and dry in the outside air. In addition to salted meat and water, hardtack

1. Myers, William Starr. *Prominent Families of New Jersey*, preview, Volumes I and II (Lewis Historical Publishing Company, 1945). Reprinted by the Genealogical Publishing Company, 2010.

2. http://www.rmg.co.uk/discover/explore/ships-biscuit

biscuits were the mainstay of a sailor's diet. Spratt was dismayed at the types of scraps stray dogs at the boatyards were eating and was inspired to create a new way to feed dogs.

While others had previously made similar biscuit-type foods, James Spratt would be the first to revolutionize commercially prepared dog foods.

From the U.K. to the USA

Spratt's new product was successful in England during the mid-to-late 1800s. In 1861, his food received a patent and became known as the Meat Fibrine Dog Cake. The baked recipe consisted of rendered meat from local bison and vegetables such as beetroot. Local ads placed in *The Sportsman*, such as the one below, dated Saturday, March 6, 1869, frequently advertised the following:

> "James Spratt, Original Inventor and Patentee of pure Fibrine Dog Cakes. They contain 20 percent of pure fibrin, the dried unsalted gelatinous parts of prairie beef, ground wheat, iron, Sulphur and charcoal. The cakes are sweetened with that great antiscorbutic and luscious fruit, the date, that never clogs or creates thirst, and substitutes vegetable. This is the cheapest food requiring no cooking, will keep your dogs in condition without meat or other food the hair glossy, the dog regular, and as a sound diet obviates worms and distemper." [sic]

In 1876, approximately four years before Spratt's death, he received another registered trademark for his Improvement in Food for Cattle (see Figure 3), a special formula that featured dates. This fruit was used to create a delicious formula that also quenched animals' thirst and was suggested to feed alongside Spratt's Fibrine Meat Dog Cakes.

UNITED STATES PATENT OFFICE.

JAMES SPRATT, OF HORSTED KEYNES, ASSIGNOR TO EDWARD WYLAM, CHARLES JOHN WYLAM, AND GEORGE BEETHAM BATCHELOR, OF SURRY COUNTY, ENGLAND.

IMPROVEMENT IN FOOD FOR CATTLE.

Specification forming part of Letters Patent No. **180,953**, dated August 8, 1876; application filed May 16, 1876.

FIGURE 3: USPTO PATENT FOR IMPROVEMENT IN FOOD FOR CATTLE

In this same year, a young man named Charles Cruft became an employee of Spratt and was quickly promoted to a salesperson. Cruft, who in later years went on to organize the famous Crufts Dog Show in London, spent a great deal of time at dog shows, providing samples of the Meat Fibrine Dog Cake to competitors and attendees alike.

Together, Spratt and Cruft set up booths and worked the dog show circuit to promote the original Meat Fibrine Dog Biscuit. Spratt's presence at these dog shows helped to form a long-lasting relationship between Spratt's Patent Ltd. and the American Kennel Club. Even after Spratt's death, the company continued to advertise their product on a regular basis in the *American Kennel Gazette*, often securing the coveted spot of magazine front cover (Figure 4).

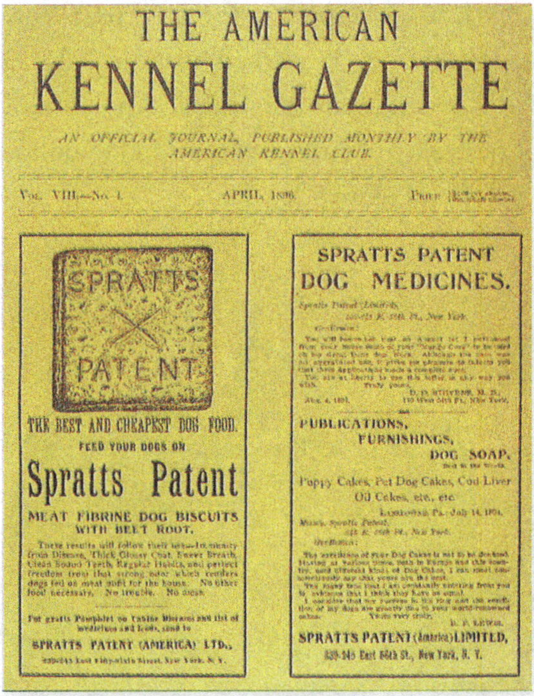
THE AMERICAN
KENNEL GAZETTE
AN OFFICIAL JOURNAL, PUBLISHED MONTHLY BY THE AMERICAN KENNEL CLUB.
APRIL, 1896
SPRATTS PATENT
THE BEST AND CHEAPEST DOG FOOD.
FEED YOUR DOGS ON
Spratts Patent
MEAT FIBRINE DOG BISCUITS WITH BEET ROOT.
SPRATTS PATENT (AMERICA) LTD.,
SPRATTS PATENT DOG MEDICINES.
PUBLICATIONS, FURNISHINGS, DOG SOAP.
Poppy Cakes, Pet Dog Cakes, Cod Liver Oil Cakes, etc., etc.
SPRATTS PATENT (America) LIMITED,

FIGURE 4: *AMERICAN KENNEL GAZETTE*
FRONT COVER, 1896

Spratt passed away around 1880. A few years before his death in 1878, he sold his company to Edward Wylam, whom he'd met through Charles Cruft. In 1885, Spratt's Patent Ltd. was registered to Edward Wylam, C.J. Wylam, and Beetham Batcheor. These three men invested 200,000 pounds between the three of them, and C.J. Wylam became the director of the organization. The company went public in 1895. The goal was to take the company to America, Russia, and Canada.

By 1893, they had quite a lucrative business. Their balance sheet showed they had 90,000 British pounds. According to *The*

Economist (1894), a spokesperson for the Spratt company stated, "The Bermondsey factory is worked to nearly the extreme limit. Further capital is required for the natural expansion of the business to provide for necessary plant, machinery and to build an additional plant at Poplar." (See Figure 5.)

FIGURE 5: SPRATTS POPLAR BISCUIT FACTORY
Photo courtesy of Fabien Egot.

To put this in perspective: 90,000 British pounds in today's USD currency and would be the equivalent of just over $42 million! This plant would eventually be recognized as the world's largest dog biscuit factory in the world. The men later opened a manufacturing plant located in New York City and established the company at No. 18 Congress Street in Newark, New Jersey. According to Charles Henry Lane's book *Dog Shows and Doggy People* (1902), even at this time in history, "individuals give practically as good care to their own animals as to themselves and members of their own families."[3]

3. Myers, William Starr. *Prominent Families of New Jersey,* preview, Volumes I and II (Lewis Historical Publishing Company, 1945). Reprinted by the Genealogical Publishing Company, 2010, page 667.

Spratt's Patent Ltd. was gaining recognition. In August of 1886, *The Weekly Northwestern Miller* newspaper noted, "Spratt's Patent Limited may claim some share in the discovery [of the north pole], as Arctic explorers are now using them for their dogs. Spratt's having supplied the two most recent expeditions—those of Walter Wellman and Dr. Nansen."

Throughout the early 1900s, Spratt's company continued to support the American Kennel Club (AKC) through advertising on their magazine covers, which gave the small organization much needed capital. Spratt's company also displayed booths at AKC dog shows (see figure 6) to promote their dog food.

FIGURE 6: PHOTO CIRCA 1908 OF SPRATT'S EXHIBITION BOOTH IN LONDON.

Spratt's Patent Ltd. had the lion's share of the market for nearly five decades,[4] until F.H. Bennett created a new product called Milk-Bone in 1908. For the first time in history, a dog biscuit became a regular item consumers purchased at the grocery store. In 1922, the Chappel Brothers of Rockford, Illinois, introduced Ken-L-Ration, the first canned dog food containing horse meat.

When the Great Depression hit, most families were forced to shift their focus to conserving money and rationing food, and dog food became a luxury. Consumers cared more about cost than quality.

During WWI, the Chappel Brothers started out supplying horses to the United States government. After the war was over, they began to export horsemeat for use in dog food. Just about the time WWII arrived, canned dog food had 90 percent of the dog food market. Metal was a critical material at this time, as the government needed it to make aircraft and other machinery, and sales of canned food nearly halted because of this. They regained a meager momentum after the war ceased. Slaughterhouses sold by-products and non-human-grade meat to dog food companies, which created a market for products that would otherwise have been discarded.

During the mid-1900s, Purina Dog Chow® became the first dog food to be made with a new extrusion technology, which is now widely used by almost all pet food manufacturers. The extrusion process consisted of combining and cooking the ingredients together in a liquid form, then mechanically pushing the mixture through the extruder, thus expanding the kibble. These kibble pieces were lighter and larger, which gave the appearance of "getting more for your money." This

---

4. Scrapes and Spratts to Specialty Diets; Caroline Coile, Ph.D. *AKC Gazette*; September 2009; 126, 9: Research Library page 18.

began the onset of clever marketing in the dog food industry, which helped in the race to promote the product to the public.

General Mills bought Spratt's Patent Ltd. in 1950 for an undisclosed amount and continued to own and operate the company until 1961. At this time, Spiller's (originally a flour milling company) acquired Spratt's for 3.94 million British pounds and later changed the name to Spratt's Patent Holdings. The name was changed again in 1972 to Spillers Food Limited.

Dr. David S. Kronfield, Paul Mellon Distinguished Professor Emeritus of Agriculture at Virginia Tech, conducted research showing too much protein was harmful to dogs. Along with other veterinarians, Dr. Kronfield proclaimed that all-meat dog foods were incomplete.[5] Pet food companies then began to label dog food as nutritionally complete. Some companies went so far as to say feeding table scraps could be dangerous and harmful to your dog's health, messaging that soon appeared in newspaper advertising.

Around the 1970s, a few celebrities begin to promote dog food on TV. Alpo had an ad featuring Lorne Greene, and Betty White promoted Science Diet. They started to show up in television advertising and gained some momentum in new markets. Some of these companies added gravy-colored food dye to make the kibble appear more natural and pleasing to the consumers' eye. Pet advertisements were beginning to emerge regularly in the media. Companies were creating new shapes and designs of pet food to be visually striking and attract the notion of being tasty. This strategy soon enabled pet food to outpace

5. Dr. Kronfield

baby food sales. Aisles and shelf space expanded enormously each year as more dog food companies joined the competition.

The next step for pet food companies was to produce specialty diets for specific diseases or disorders. Dr. Mark Morris, DVM and founder of Hill's Pet Products™, first came up with this notion in a product now called Science Diet™. Following suit in this endeavor was Purina™. Veterinarians championed these products, which were only available for purchase through a veterinary office.

Companies such as Hill's soon started portraying dog food nutrition as complex, and the public began to rely on their veterinarian's advice about pet nutrition. Veterinarians soon gained notoriety as nutrition experts with the advent of prescription pet food, which implied that nutrition was sophisticated.

In 1974, the National Research Council developed a protocol for nutritional values needed in pet food. That same year, the American Association of Feed Control Officials (AAFCO) was formed, the first group to help regulate what went into pet food.

Former Spratt employee Chris Norman wrote in his personal memoirs of his time working at Spratt's in 1972, "The company I worked for from 1972 was Spratt's Patent Ltd. . . . based in Cambridge Road, Barking, Essex. The company had been acquired by Spillers but was still being run as a separate company."

This information was part of a major discovery the authors of this book made regarding the ownership of Nutro.

Chris went on to say, "Spillers had their own pet food grocery division, but this was run as a competitor . . . I didn't understand this concept originally but began to realise that competition for shelf space was critical and by running two companies side by side you could gain double this shelf space."[6] Even four decades earlier, the concept of shelf space was being talked about and still is today.

The late 1900s saw "premium" dog foods as the newest trend in commercial pet food. Companies advertised their premium foods as being more nutritious for dogs and offered various blends for all stages of life, including puppy, maintenance, performance, and senior foods. Despite the premium labels, many of these companies were using old nutritional requirements from the 1970s. They could also sell these premium foods for a premium price, since consumers considered the ingredients and formulations to be more expensive. Some companies claimed to have superior ingredients, yet these same ingredients appeared on the labels of grocery-brand dog food.

Consumers nowadays have become more educated on nutrition not only for themselves, but for their pets as well. Many consumers began to read labels to sort out what the best food *truly* was. Because companies need to include preservatives to extend the life of the kibble, they began using chemicals like ethoxyquin, BHA, and BHT, which didn't sit well with many dog owners. Consumers began to refuse to buy from companies using these potentially cancer-causing ingredients,[7] along with products containing corn and corn by-products.

The new millennium brought even more changes in the industry. Over the end of the last decade, natural pet food became a focus in pet food labeling. Companies began to make official statements

---

6. Grace's Guide to British Industrial History: http://www.gracesguide.co.uk/Spratt's_Patent

7. http://ntp.niehs.nih.gov/ntp/roc/content/profiles/butylatedhydroxyanisole.pdf

about being organic and containing human-grade ingredients. By now, consumers generally want meat as the first ingredient, yet many companies are still producing food with upward of 50 percent grain, fillers, and grain by-products.

The infamous pet food recall of 2007 sent consumers into a frenzy about food safety and quality for their beloved dogs and cats. In this devastating incident, manufacturers unknowingly purchased wheat gluten tainted with melamine—a material widely used in plastics, adhesives, and dishware and *not* in pet food—from a supplier in China. When the melamine was used in wheat gluten, it created a higher protein level content, thus making the wheat gluten appear to be a high-quality ingredient. The Food and Drug Administration (FDA) issued an alert on March 15, 2007, that certain foods were making pets sick and some were dying from the tainted food.

One unnamed pet food manufacturer contacted the FDA to alert them to the fact that 14 dogs and cats had perished while eating their food containing the suspected melamine. The death of pets was far greater than this one report. Unfortunately, when pets began to consume it, it had fatal results. This impact was felt by all pet food manufacturers, including Nutro; it hampered the company's bottom line as it approached the $800 million mark.

This incident, along with several other recalls, prompted consumers to become fearful about feeding their pets. As a result, manufacturers had to go to great lengths to determine the origins of the ingredients they purchased. Many manufacturers began claiming their food was made in the USA. Some even put American flags on bags of pet food.

Dogs have gone from the barnyard to the backyard and finally to the bedroom. Small dog ownership is on the rise, and pets are now commonly traveling companions for their parents. According to a 2016 Gallup Poll, 76 percent of Americans have given their pet a present on Christmas, and 60 percent of pet owners believe owning a pet leads to a more satisfying lifestyle compared to non-pet owners.[8] We see people pushing their dogs in strollers, and pet-related clothing is trendy and fashionable. When the Great Recession hit in 2009-2010, the amount of money people spent eating out declined sharply, yet the purchases of pet food stayed constant.

Celebrity endorsements of pet-related items from people like Martha Stewart are becoming more prevalent. Former PetSmart CEO Bob Moran said, "The natural, organic trend is going to keep on getting bigger and bigger. We're also matching up with new vendors, new assortments, even proprietary brands . . . We have product partnerships with Martha Stewart, [Poison lead singer and reality-TV star] Bret Michaels, GNC, Marvel Comics, Toys 'R' Us. About three and a half years ago, about 15 percent of product sales came from exclusive PetSmart products. Today, they're around 23 percent."[9]

Pets are woven into the fabric of our lives. With over 75 percent of American households owning a pet,[10] it is no wonder that the future of the pet industry has a very bright outlook.

8. http://www.gallup.com/poll/25969/Americans-Their-Pets.aspx

9. http://www.l3corp.net/2012/robert-moran-ceo-of-petsmart-inc-on-how-the-family-dog-has-become-a-family-member/

10. http://www.bls.gov/opub/btn/volume-2/spending-on-pets.htm

3

Building the Empire

"If you work just for money, you'll never make it, but if you love what you're doing and you always put the customer first, success will be yours."

—Ray Kroc

According to two leading analysts at GfK (*Gesellschaft für Konsumforschung* Society for Consumer Research), the fourth largest market research organization in the world, global retail pet food sales have reached over a staggering $70 billion.[11]

Of the $70 billion, North America composes the largest spending continent, pulling in nearly 30 percent of the total alone. In 2010, pet food outsold baby food by 160 percent, and by 133 percent in 2015. Pet food was $59.3 billion in 2010 and $73.3 billion in 2015. Global pet food sales are significantly higher than baby food revenue.

11. http://www.petfoodindustry.com/blogs/7-adventures-in-pet-food/post/5609-global-pet-food-trends-sales-and-volume-rose-4-in-2015

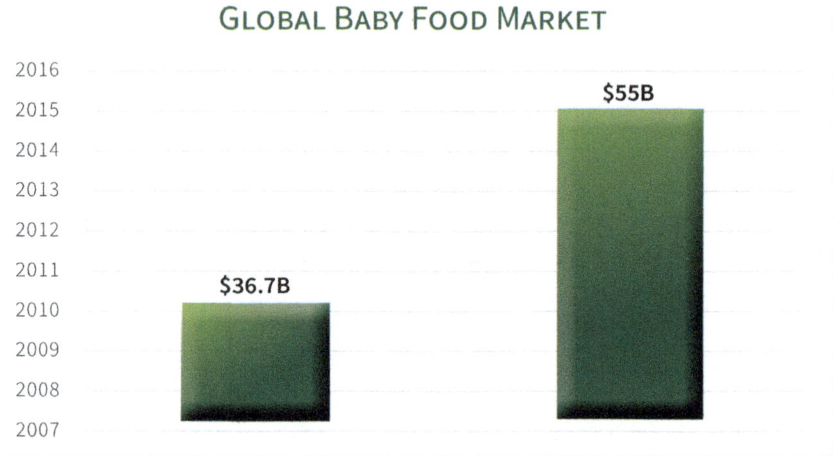

TABLE 1
Source: Euromonitor, 2015.

Over 131 million babies are born annually throughout the world.[12] Each is a potential consumer of baby food. Yet surprisingly, global sales of pet food have shot past baby food sales by *$15 billion*. A study conducted in 2012[13] by the American Veterinary Medical Association (AVMA) showed more than 75 percent of U.S. households own a dog or cat. U.S. households alone are responsible for owning more than 140 million dogs and cats, therefore making the pet food industry a powerhouse of consumer packaged goods.

So which companies are selling all this food? There are several notable (and usual) suspects, such as Colgate-Palmolive (Hill's), Mars, and Nestle, but one major player, Procter & Gamble (P&G), is missing from the list these days. The world's top 10 pet food companies are represented in annual revenue as follows in Table 2.

12. http://www.ecology.com/birth-death-rates/

13. https://www.avma.org/KB/Resources/Statistics/Pages/Market-research-statistics-US-pet-ownership.aspx

COMPANY	COUNTRY	ANNUAL REVENUE
Mars Petcare, Inc.	USA	$17,224,400,000
Nestle Purina PetCare	USA	$11,917,000,000
Big Heart Pet Brands	USA	$2,280,300,000
Hill's Pet Nutrition	USA	$2,212,000,000
Diamond Pet Foods	USA	$1,150,00 0,000
Blue Buffalo	USA	$1,027,447,000
Spectrum Brands/ United Pet Group	USA	$800,000,000
Unicharm Corp.	JAPAN	$722,565,401
Deuerer	GERMANY	$721,100,000
Heristo AG	GERMANY	$700,000,000
TOTAL		$38,754,812,401

TABLE 2

Source: Petfood Industry 2017 data, PetfoodIndustry.com

Out of the top 10 companies, Mars Petcare ascended to the top with their 2014 P&G acquisition. Thanks to a $2.9 billion all-cash deal, Mars, a privately held company ranked fifth on Forbes' List of America's Largest Private Companies, bought Procter & Gamble's pet food business. According to Reuters,[14] the transaction handed over the reins of 80 percent of the U.S. and select foreign countries pet food business.

Table 3 shows the various brands these companies feature. You'll likely recognize some names, but many large private and publicly traded companies have been buying up smaller, independently owned pet food companies.

14. http://www.reuters.com/article/us-mars-pgpetcare-acquisition-idUSBREA3811O20140409

MANUFACTURER	BRANDS
Mars Petcare, Inc.	Nutro, Iams, Eukanuba, Greenies, California Natural, Innova, Pedigree, Little Whiskas, Cesar, Royal Canin
Nestle Purina PetCare	Alpo, Bakers, Beneful, Purina, Chef Michael's, Purina ONE, Friskies, Fancy Feast, Merrick, Felix, Castor & Pollux
Big Heart Pet Brands	Nature's Recipe, Milk-Bone, Kibbles 'n Bits, Gravy Train, Nine Lives, Meow Mix, Alley Cat
Hill's Pet Nutrition	Science Diet
Diamond Pet Foods	Natural Balance, Diamond Naturals, CANIDAE, Chicken Soup, Country Value, Kirkland, Premium Edge, Professional, Solid Gold, Taste of the Wild
Blue Buffalo	BLUE Basics, BLUE Freedom, BLUE Wilderness, BLUE Life Protection Formula
Spectrum Brands/ United Pet Group	DreamBone, SmartBones, Better Belly, Good 'N' Fun, 8in1, Wild Harvest, Dingo
Unicharm Corp.	Aiken Genki, Neko Genki, Gaines, Gin no Spoon, and Gin no Sara
Deuerer	Private label manufacturer
Heristo AG	Saturn Petcare, Animonda Petcare

TABLE 3

BRANDS OWNED BY MANUFACTURERS AS OF AUGUST 2016

Source: company websites.

The first major shift in this trend was the sale of the Iams Company. Much like Nutro, Iams touted the fact that consumers could only find their products in pet specialty stores, not grocery or mass markets. Then in 1999, Iams owner Clay Mathile decided to sell his company to P&G. The owners of Nutro made a similar decision in May of 2007, when Mars purchased Nutro for over $2 billion. In Clay Mathile's book, *Dream No Little Dreams*, he refers to the top three premium pet food companies as "Hills, Iams, and Nutro."[15]

You might have noticed that we refer to people with pets as "pet parents." These are not just a dog or cat "owner." Consumers treat their canine and feline companions as members of the family. In fact, statistics tell us that two-thirds of pet owners would spend any amount and even go into debt to save the life of their pet.[16] According to the American Pet Products Association 2010-2011 Pet Survey,[17] "over $11,000 will be spent on the lifetime of a [dog], even in times of a recession."

Consider these other statistics[18] on what pet owners think and do:

- 57 percent of pet owners surveyed would want a pet as their *only* companion if deserted on an island.
- 80 percent of survey respondents selected companionship as the major reason for having a pet.
- 72 percent of pet owners say that affection is their pet's most endearing trait.
- 79 percent of surveyed pet owners give their pets holiday or birthday presents.
- 33 percent of pet owners talk to their pets on the phone or through the answering machine.

---

15. Mathile, Clayton, and Echo, Garr. *Dream No Little Dreams* (DNLD Publishing, 2008).

16. https://faunalytics.org/feature-article/most-pet-owners-will-spend-anything-to-save-pets-life-survey-says/

17. https://faunalytics.org/feature-article/2011-2012-appa-national-pet-owners-survey/

18. https://faunalytics.org/wp-content/uploads/2015/05/Citation1338.pdf

- 62 percent of respondents often sign letters or cards from them and their pets.
- 55 percent of pet owners consider themselves as mom or dad to their pets.

Even decades before these results, the leadership at Nutro saw this wave of pet ownership becoming an increasingly integral part of every American's daily life. Nutro had been floating steadily out at sea for years, and the company was primed to finish building the empire when the 1990s rolled around. The organization was able to connect with consumers and create a powerful demand for their pet food, and they capitalized on this connection, along with the love affair people have with their pets.

4

The Lineage: From Mustang to Milky Way

"The quality of a person's life is in direct proportion to their commitment to excellence, regardless of their chosen field of endeavor."
—Vince Lombardi

John C. Saleen was born on April 6, 1918, in the small town of WaKeeney, Kansas, to a family who grew wheat and raised cattle on their family farm. John's grandfather, Olaf, had emigrated from Sweden with his parents before the turn of the century. John's parents at some point decided to move the family west, and eventually settled in Redondo Beach, California.

John was drafted into the Air Force in 1941 and served his country honorably during World War II (see Figure 7). Upon his entry into the Army, John had a strong desire to be a pilot. After all, he already had his pilot's license. Unfortunately, the colorblindness discovered during his physical entry examination prevented him from this endeavor. His youngest son Mike explains, "My dad was crushed to hear this."

FIGURE 7: PHOTO CIRCA 1944
Photo courtesy of Robyn Saleen.

Instead, John was assigned to be a crew member aboard B-17 and B-25 bombers as a radio operator, engineer, tail gunner, and morse code reader. He was stationed in the Pacific Corridor and called Guam and the Philippines home for several years. Mike proudly yet humbly shared, "My dad was not the type of person to talk about his war service unless he was asked about it. He completed 75 missions fighting the Japanese—[and he] *volunteered* for the majority of these. His squadron was one of the lucky ones to survive the war and make it back home." Right after Japan surrendered the war, John's squadron flew their bomber home.

Steve, the eldest of John's three children, vividly recalls his father telling him of their return from Japan. As Steve was telling me (Christie) this story, he sat back in his chair, folded his arms behind his head, and smiled as he shared, "My father was a tail gunner and the crew decided they wanted to fly underneath the Golden Gate Bridge in San Francisco on their way returning to home base. They thought they might get in trouble; but hell, the war was over and they were happy to be alive. It was one last hurrah."

John served honorably after arriving home as an instructor for B-29s at March Air Force base in Riverside, California. During the time John was serving in the Air Force, his Uncle Herman started his own business, Pacific Dog Catering Company (see Figure 8). This draft registration card shows the relationship between Herman Saleen and his company, Pacific Dog Catering.

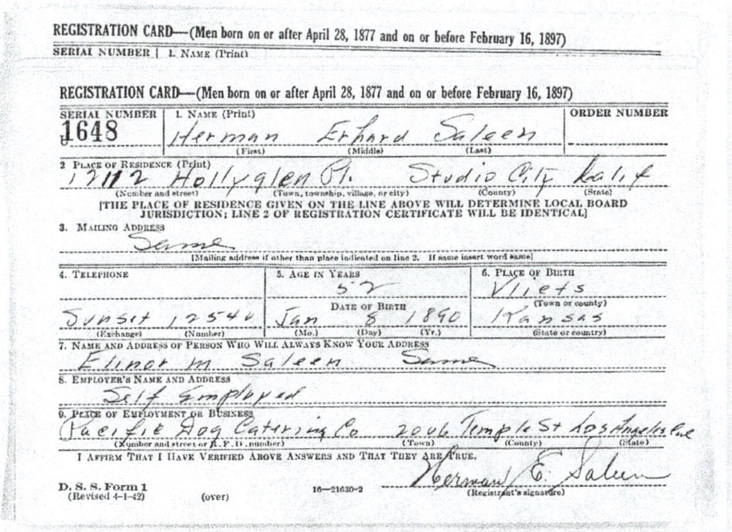

REGISTRATION CARD—(Men born on or after April 28, 1877 and on or before February 16, 1897)
SERIAL NUMBER | 1. NAME (Print)

REGISTRATION CARD—(Men born on or after April 28, 1877 and on or before February 16, 1897)

SERIAL NUMBER 1648 | 1. NAME (Print) Herman Erhard Saleen (First) (Middle) (Last) | ORDER NUMBER

2 PLACE OF RESIDENCE (Print) 17112 Hollyglen Pl. Studio City Calif (Number and street) (Town, township, village, or city) (County) (State)

[THE PLACE OF RESIDENCE GIVEN ON THE LINE ABOVE WILL DETERMINE LOCAL BOARD JURISDICTION; LINE 2 OF REGISTRATION CERTIFICATE WILL BE IDENTICAL]

3. MAILING ADDRESS Same
[Mailing address if other than place indicated on line 2. If same insert word same]

4. TELEPHONE Sunset 12540 (Exchange) (Number) | 5. AGE IN YEARS 52 DATE OF BIRTH Jan 8 1890 (Mo.) (Day) (Yr.) | 6. PLACE OF BIRTH Vliets (Town or county) Kansas (State or country)

7. NAME AND ADDRESS OF PERSON WHO WILL ALWAYS KNOW YOUR ADDRESS Elinor M. Saleen Same

8. EMPLOYER'S NAME AND ADDRESS Self Employed

9. PLACE OF EMPLOYMENT OR BUSINESS Pacific Dog Catering Co 2006 Temple St Los Angeles Calif (Number and street or R.F.D. number) (Town) (County) (State)

I AFFIRM THAT I HAVE VERIFIED ABOVE ANSWERS AND THAT THEY ARE TRUE.

D. S. S. Form 1 (Revised 4-1-42) (over) 16—21630-2 Herman E. Saleen (Registrant's signature)

FIGURE 8: HERMAN ERHARD SALEEN DRAFT CARD
Resourced from www.genealogy.com

Herman left WaKeeney in 1933 to start his new operation. Later, Albert, Herman's brother and John Saleen's father, sold the family farm and headed west to join his brother. Albert helped his brother Herman with the fox farm business. Herman (Figure 9) taught his brother everything he knew about raising foxes and operating a fox farm. Herman also had a side business selling wet dog food. He owned his own slaughterhouse, which helped him in making the food.

Figure 9: Herman Erhard Saleen Resourced from www.genealogy.com

Herman later developed a "meatloaf" type of fox food, which he determined would be excellent for dogs as well, since it made their coats shiny and soft. Herman used to sell the meatloaf to a variety of customers and made these deliveries in his company vehicle (Figure 10). Herman sold his wet food to a company that would later end up being purchased by Kal-Kan®.

FIGURE 10: HERMAN ERHARD SALEEN'S DELIVERY VEHICLE
Resourced from www.genealogy.com

After John was honorably discharged from the Air Force, he decided to remain in Southern California to live near his parents. He joined a youth organization at the local church called Luther League. During a function one evening, John met a beautiful young woman named Evelyn. They were married on October 13, 1945, and lived in Whittier. They were founding members of a local Lutheran church, whose congregation they belonged to for the next 50 years. John and Evelyn's daughter Robyn lovingly recalls, "Dad was an avid reader and loved Western novels, reading poetry, and watching golf and auto racing. People looked to my dad as an example of how to live an honest life and he took very good care of other people. He was the everyman's man."

While John held several jobs after the military, none of the positions seemed to provide anything he was passionate about. It wasn't too long before Herman asked his nephew John if he would like to manage his delivery route for Pacific Dog Catering for a few weeks while he went out of town. During this time, John found his purpose. He quickly became an advocate for animals and had a yearning to be involved in pet nutrition. John and his Uncle Herman became business partners in the Pacific Dog Food Catering Company (Figure 11).

FIGURE 11: STOREFRONT OF PACIFIC DOG CATERING & NUTRO DOG FOOD
Photo credit: Mike and Desi Saleen.

Mike Saleen said, "I think it must have been my Uncle Herman who owned Nutro Dog Food. We don't have any documents and I was not even born yet. My wife, Desi, recalls my mom telling us that she and my dad bought a small house in October of 1945 for the purpose of [what we'd now call] 'flipping' it. The $500 they made on the house became the down payment for the business my father wanted to buy from Uncle Herman. The house was sold in April of 1947."

While reviewing old documents with Steve Saleen, we can see business transactions regarding Nutro equipment that validates what Mike recalls. According to the USPTO (United States Patent and Trademark Office), John Saleen renewed the Nutro Dog Food Company trademark in 1952 from the family of Herben Serois.

Serois had started the company in 1931 and received approval to use the trademark Nutro™ in 1936.

Little has been recorded on Herben Serois (Figure 12) and his ownership of the Nutro Dog Food Company. We know that he was born on July 31, 1879, in Kankakee, Illinois, to parents Anthony Serois and Josephine Levegue. They had two sons: Edwin, born in 1884, and Herben. According to Herben's WWII draft card, we can see that he had brown hair, brown eyes, and was 5'6" tall. We have been unable to locate any other photos of Herben or his family. Herben appears to have been married twice: first to Dalia, with whom he had two sons, Clyde and Byron, and later to Vivian, who was 12 years his junior. Vivian was 50 when Herben passed away on October 2, 1942. They had no children, although Vivian had a son, Curtis.

Herben Serois

Funeral services for Herben Serois, 63, a dog food manufacturer, who died Friday at his home, 2617 Waverly Drive, will be conducted at 2:30 p.m. tomorrow at the Wee Kirk o' the Heather. Interment will be in Forest Lawn Memorial Park. Serois leaves his widow, Mrs. Vivian Serois, a brother, Edwin Serois, St. Anne, Ill., and three sisters, Mrs. Lilly Denno, Monett, Mo., Mrs. Flossy Beisz, Peotone, Ill., and Mrs. Aurora Adams, Toledo, O.

FIGURE 12: HERBEN SEROIS OBITUARY
Resourced from www.genealogy.com
Los Angeles Times, *October 4, 1942.*

Based on limited newspaper articles, it did appear as though Herben was fairly active in the pet industry. The *Hollywood Citizen News* cited in an article with no author listed, "Dog lovers [proclaimed] the Ventura County Dog Fanciers' Association first annual show in 1935[19] . . . as one of the most successful shows ever presented in Southern California . . . The show was one of the best ever . . . according to H. Serois, manufacturer of a nationally known dog food, who attends all the dog shows."

19. https://vcdfa.weebly.com/history.html

Later, John Saleen went on to purchase other micro pet-care companies such as Barnett, Mackall's, and Krill. Eventually, these all rolled up into the Nutro Dog Food Company. In 1963, seeking to add to his company, John sent the letter shown in Figure 13 to Spratt's in an effort to use their name in the U.S. This letter would have been the first contact John Saleen made with the Spratt's company to use their name. No other documentation has been found to gauge the response from the English company, and John never sold Spratt's in the U.S.

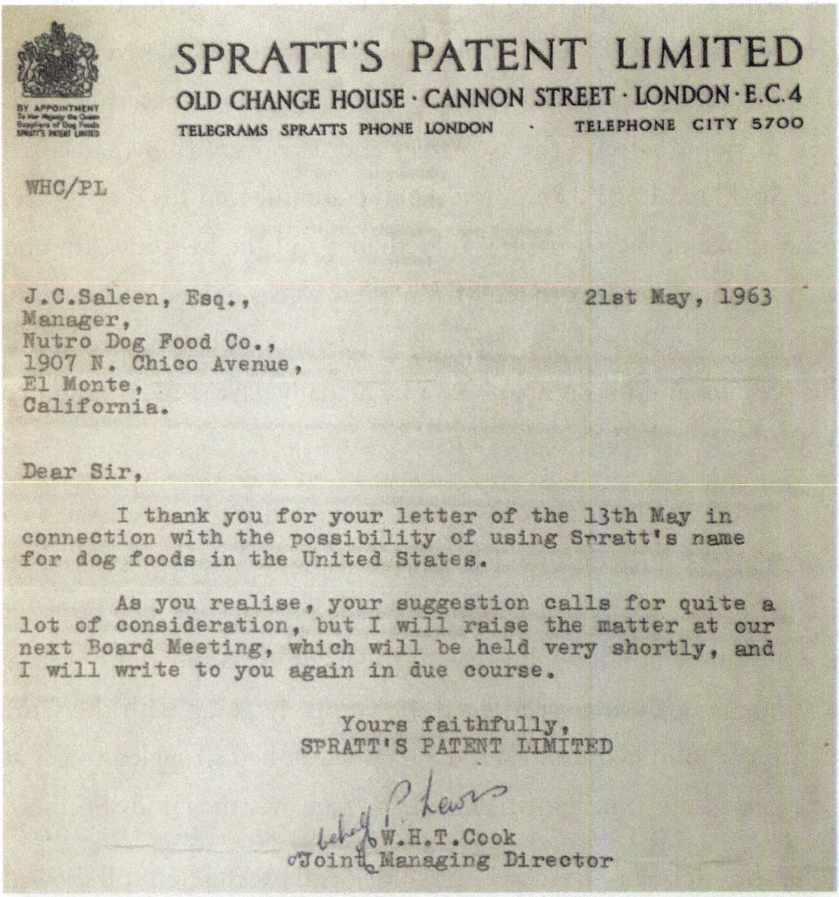

SPRATT'S PATENT LIMITED
OLD CHANGE HOUSE · CANNON STREET · LONDON · E.C.4
TELEGRAMS SPRATTS PHONE LONDON · TELEPHONE CITY 5700

WHC/PL

J.C.Saleen, Esq., 21st May, 1963
Manager,
Nutro Dog Food Co.,
1907 N. Chico Avenue,
El Monte,
California.

Dear Sir,

I thank you for your letter of the 13th May in connection with the possibility of using Srratt's name for dog foods in the United States.

As you realise, your suggestion calls for quite a lot of consideration, but I will raise the matter at our next Board Meeting, which will be held very shortly, and I will write to you again in due course.

Yours faithfully,
SPRATT'S PATENT LIMITED

W.H.T.Cook
Joint Managing Director

FIGURE 13: LETTER TO SPRATT'S TO ACQUIRE NAME FOR USE IN UNITED STATES
Document courtesy of Mike Saleen.

While John Saleen had no formal college education, he was a self-taught chemist with a knack for formulating dog food. John was the one to formulate the pet food and other Nutro supplements the company produced. Natural nutrition was a critical component in making these products, and John was considered a pioneer in creating health foods for pets. Saleen's active involvement in the pet industry compelled him to attend pet trade shows regularly. One particular trade show proved to be a pivotal moment in John's life.

Ed Brown, a sales representative for Lee Mar, a distributor of pet related hard goods, was attending a local pet industry convention in 1973 when he strategically placed himself at a table to eat his lunch next to John Saleen. The two men had a conversation that lasted the entire meal as Ed inquired why he should feed his dog Nutro. John spoke of the all-natural ingredients and the lustrous skin and coat Ed should expect to see within a few weeks of feeding Nutro to his dog. Ed was so mesmerized by the passion John showed about his product and his company that he actually gave some thought to what it would be like to be Nutro's owner.

The ensuing years led to occasional conversations between the two solopreneurs. Ed continued to ponder how he could raise enough capital to buy the company *and* persuade John to sell it to him. Ed consistently reminded John that members of his family did not have a strong enough interest to keep the company going with the same passion as John had, but Ed did. John Saleen had struggled to get at least one of this three grown children to take over the family business.

John's health began to fail as he got older, and his children still showed no interest in operating Nutro Products. In 1975, John decided to have one last conversation with his three grown children about running the business after he retired. Middle child Mike was intrigued by law; he would go on to graduate from Whittier College and attend Loyola to earn his law degree. Robyn, the youngest of the kids, ran a pet store; and the oldest son, Steve, was interested in racing cars.

Of all John's three children, Steve Saleen had spent the most time in the family business. Both Steve and his younger brother, Mike, spent summer and non-school days working for their father. Steve and Mike both speak fondly and remember well the days when they would drive to one of three bread stores in the area.

FIGURE 14: NUTRO DOG FOOD COMPANY BUILDING
Photo courtesy of Steve Saleen.

Steve revealed, "My father would drive me and my brother to Langendorf, Helm, or Weber's Bread to purchase wheat bread to use as an ingredient in our products. My dad would drive the Ford station wagon along with a wooden flatbed with metal siding to pick up the bread weekly. Once we got back to the plant, my brother and I would unload the bread [Figure 14]. We'd play around a bit and we would jump from the roof of the station wagon and land onto the pillows of Wonder Bread beneath us. What fun days!"

Mike emphasized, "Our dad analyzed the dog food we made and wanted to make sure we were making and selling health food for dogs. In doing his research, he found that Langendorf Bakery used a superior [brand of] flour as an ingredient, and that's why we used their bread in our early formulation."

Steve eventually decided to attend USC and major in business. He went on to graduate in 1971. As Steve grew up, he found himself participating more in the family business he'd come to know so well. He helped in making the food and conducting deliveries, and after graduating college, he was assigned to be a temporary salesman for Vern, an employee who recently had a heart attack and could not work. Temporary soon turned into permanent for the next several years, and Steve set out to make his mark in the pet industry.

Steve quickly discovered that a lot of pet food retailers did not have good marketing tactics. Regional malls were being developed at this time, and many of these malls featured pet stores. So Steve decided to go back to school and take some post-graduate classes. In one of his courses, designed to allow students to learn how to lay out stores and create merchandising plans, Steve recalled, "I remember I was sitting next to the president at Ralphs supermarket!" Steve admired the fact that a person of the president's stature was present.

Steve combined the merchandising schematics he learned with his own ideas and created plan-o-grams to make the most of the pet shops to whom Nutro was selling. He was instrumental in developing these initial formal marketing ideas for Nutro as they began to control more of the retailers' growth.

Steve recalled, "I was single at the time and therefore able to dedicate much time to helping the retailers in Southern California grow their business. We would take small, unorganized stores, plan out their shelving, and create a beautiful, well organized store that made sense to the shopper. I realized it felt like I was working 24/7 and often late: nine, ten, eleven o'clock at night. We were controlling a lot of what the store was doing and our business was really flourishing."

During this time in the mid-70s, Nutro's business was not just manufacturing; it also included distributing hard goods for pets like flea control products, fish supplies, and many others.

Steve had other impacts on his father's dog food manufacturing business, like collaborating on the creation of the Nutro logo (although this occurred shortly after his father sold Nutro.) The Saleens also owned retail pet and feed stores that Steve helped to set up, the first of which was Pet Barn in Sacramento, California. Since Steve was the eldest of the three Saleen kids, John leaned on him quite a bit to help run much of the day-to-day operations.

As he found his compass and his true north in life, Steve became very passionate about cars and racing *and* his soon-to-be wife. As Steve reflected, he admitted, "Between dog food and cars, cars were my first love." For years, he went back and forth between racing and dog food. His passion for pet food eventually waned, while his passion for cars steadily rose. Steve found that he was truly at his best when racing cars. Eventually, he had the opportunity as well as his wife's blessing and support to make his mark in the automotive industry. In 1983, Steve founded Saleen Autosport.

John Saleen eventually realized his children did not have the same calling to continue with Nutro that he had. When he struck out with all three, John called Ed Brown and said, "Put a price on it and let's chat."

5

A Leap of Faith

> ***"Faith is to believe what you do not yet see; the reward for this faith is to see what you believe."***
> *—St. Augustine*

In 1975, the average cost of a home was $43,400,[20] and the average American's income was barely topping $16,000. A postage stamp was a dime, a loaf of bread was just a quarter, and a tank of gas for the average car was less than $10. So when Ed Brown went home and asked his wife, "Honey, we can build an incredible future we have always wanted for $300,000. What do you think?" Her reply was one of support; yet she gently encouraged her husband that it might be in their best interest to find a business partner.

Ed was born on February 23, 1927, in Duluth, Minnesota. He met his wife, Geraldine, on a blind date when they were both 16 years old. Six years later, the couple was married when Ed was a senior at the University of Minnesota, majoring in business and economics.

---

20. http://www.census.gov/const/uspricemon

Before asking Geraldine's father for her hand in marriage, he devised a plan to save up $1,000 for their honeymoon. After he saved the money, Ed spoke to Geri's father and mentioned he was a very rich man. Ed fondly recalls, "I fell madly in love with her. She was the cutest thing in the world." As of 2016, they had been married 73 years, and Ed confessed, "I love her more and more every day and I don't know where it keeps coming from."

One reason is likely her wisdom and insight, since Geri provided some good advice that day in 1975. Ed agreed with his wife, then called up a dear friend of his named Don Taffy, who worked with a professional management group, to discuss this business opportunity. Ed told Don, "I am looking for a person with the right stuff to help build a pet food empire." Don made several phone calls and had someone of particular interest he thought would be best suited for Ed to collaborate with.

Just like when two ingredients come together, certain partnerships are immensely successful. Consider how the truly revolutionary combination of peanut butter and chocolate made the world-famous Reese's Peanut Butter Cup™. This is precisely what happened when Ed Brown and David Traitel decided to join forces. They were two ingredients that, when combined, forever changed the pet industry.

And so began this very successful partnership between the two. Some people wondered how two such driven individuals could manage the business and not let egos get in the way. But the answer was simple, really: they each took charge of the area that suited their strengths.

Ed was the relationship-builder, and easily created a market by just asking one simple question: "So tell me, Tiger, does your dog have hot spots or dry, itchy skin?" Ed truly had a gift for making his customers feel as if each was the most important and *only* person in the world. He didn't have to work hard at being heartfelt and genuine; he exuded authenticity and honesty, and it emanated from him everywhere he went.

David was the visionary. According to one past CEO, "David had an uncanny ability to see into the future, much like a Steve Jobs." Another marketing manager emphasized, "Dave's level of integrity, honesty, financial acumen, and ability to be a wholesome and genuine individual made him the ideal leader for managing the financial and strategic aspects of the company."

Dave once wrote, "Great companies are seldom constructed around any particular product. They are instead enrobed by a design. A product has a finite lifetime due to the competitive forces of the marketplace. Conversely, a properly conceived corporate design contains within its nucleus a self-regeneration potential. This enables an organization to transcend the vagaries of product-based competition."

It is this design, which includes strategy and culture, that interests us as authors most. Qualitative surveys, distributed to many associated with the Nutro business who were hired before 2007, have explored issues around this design, and we've conducted a great deal of personal interviews with stakeholders.

6

Trees Don't Grow to the Sky

"Whoever sows sparingly will also reap sparingly, and whoever sows generously will reap generously."
—2 Corinthians 9:6

In the early years of the partnership between Ed and Dave, Nutro consistently saw growth in the 30-40% range, which was quite impressive for such a young company. Knowing that this type of growth could not be sustained over a long period, Dave Traitel used to say, "Trees don't grow to the sky." In other words, he knew it might be time to recalculate the growth they were expecting and the goals they were setting for the company, since 40% might be a bit *too* high to continue.

While Dave certainly wanted his company to do well, he also knew the importance of being realistic. The strategies that grew from the design of the company were based on what the organization has repeatedly called "belly-to-belly" selling: being in front of people who needed to be educated on the product and understand the benefits to using Nutro.

Nutro employed four main belly-to-belly strategies up until the mid-2000s. According to one past president of the company, "There was no need to be first." Those with a competitive nature might wonder why, but the short- and long-term goal was one and the same, and was simple: sell one bag at a time.

This might seem like a rather slow way to ramp up and gain market share and sales. And Nutro didn't share any lengthy company blueprints or five-year plans. Their tactic was to employ straightforward strategies, thereby allowing the company to be nimble and out-maneuver the competition, an approach that ultimately proved incredibly successful.

These four major strategies, shown in Figure 15, were the center of the organization. Its members unanimously agreed to the following strategies:

1. Sell on the differential.
2. Sell by conversion.
3. Gain recommendation.
4. Sell belly-to-belly using the best people.

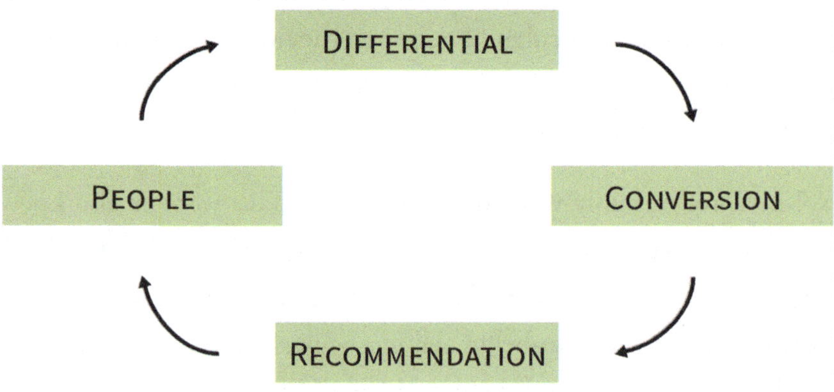

FIGURE 15: BELLY-TO-BELLY STRATEGIES OF NUTRO

These might not be glamorous strategic approaches, but they allowed a company to go from zero to $800 million in two decades *without* the financial assistance of banks or venture capitalists. Each element of this approach played an integral part in Nutro's success.

7

Belly-to-Belly Strategy #1: Differential

> ***"Success is not measured by what you do compared to what others do. It is measured by what you do with the ability God gave you."***
> *—Zig Ziglar*

American academic Michael Porter, known for his theories on business strategies, said, "A company can outperform rivals only if it can establish a difference it can preserve." The difference for Nutro was two-fold: the product's ingredients, and the fact that it was only sold in pet specialty outlets, not supermarkets.

This difference was referred to fondly with the slogan, "The Difference Is Nutrition"™ and was the message Nutro used to go to market and to sell everyone on this differential. It did not matter if it was an employee in accounting, sales, manufacturing, marketing, or other team; every member of the company was passionately selling the product.

> ***It was common for Nutro team members to "convert" consumers in a variety of places: on airplanes, in line at the grocery store, and of course, in conversations with friends and family.***

The ingredient differential was something that most of the "big guys"—competitors like Hill's and Procter & Gamble—were not using. In fact, they were working arduously to go to market and battle with their "me-too" ingredients. Nutro first used the differential strategy in the mid-50s, under previous owner John Saleen. John's love of nutrition and chemistry allowed him to create Nutro's "all-natural" products. Nutro later hired a young, bright, and headstrong nutritional authority named Dr. Sharon Machlik, who joined the company to create a new line of cat food. Instead, Dr. Machlik began to enhance a product line called Max™, which launched in 1977 and contributed significantly to the company's early success. Max's ingredients, or rather, lack thereof, became the company mantra for decades: "No heads, no feet, no guts."

The big guys *were* selling heads, feet, and guts in their ingredient decks, so Nutro began to use this ingredient differential in all recipes moving forward. Dr. Macklik was passionate about research, the equipment, and the process. She created a proprietary blend of ingredients that the company was able to use 15 years before anyone else had even considered taking a similar approach, truly putting Nutro ahead of the pack.

The difference allowed Nutro to bring superior value to the consumer, which made Nutro's competitors easy to sell against. Nutro used chicken meal instead of poultry by-products, rice instead of ground yellow corn, and sunflower oil rather than animal fat. The company could sell these premium ingredients at a premium price in comparison to the substitute ingredients that the competition offered. Consumers could feed less of the product to their pets, since it was more digestible, and the fat source created a shinier skin and coat, which meant less shedding. This unique combination was Nutro's main selling strategy. Of the recipes created after Max, the foremost impact was Natural Choice Lamb and Rice™. In fact, most executives at Nutro would agree that in 1991 the creation of Natural Choice Lamb and Rice was the tipping point for Nutro.

The company was able to continue their differential tactic by making power claims about the product's performance. Statements like "guaranteed to improve skin and coat" made the product "bullet-proof," a term Nutro employees commonly used to indicate the product was always reliable, unbreakable, and impervious to failure.

The success of Max made way for other formula creations at Nutro. The creations that came after Natural Choice were *all* assembled by Dr. Gary Crosslin, a quiet man with a brilliant mind. Just like Dr. Sharon Machlik, Dr. Crosslin had an enormous blend of talents. He knew the intricacies of how ingredients would behave in the extruders, as well as each ingredient's digestibility and palatability. After receiving test results from vice president of technical services Rudy Leschke and his team of technical advisors, Drs. Crosslin and Machlik knew precisely what to change in the formula to enhance performance, palatability, and digestibility, every time. The entire research and development team worked tirelessly on implementing and perfecting processes to improve the testing on all products, making the product even *more* bullet-proof.

These power claims allowed retailers to sell the product successfully as well, which went a long way in the second aspect of the differential strategy: the fact that Nutro was only available in pet specialty stores. Most pet food sales were coming primarily from grocery and mass markets, back in the late 70s. This meant that Nutro needed to change not just the brand a consumer was shopping for but also consumers' shopping *patterns.* Asking a pet owner to buy Nutro would require them to make an additional stop to pick up Fido's food, and that was where the next strategy came in.

8

Belly-to-Belly Strategy #2: Conversion

"If you can't feed a hundred people, then feed just one."
—*Mother Teresa*

Selling by conversion, also known as "selling one bag at a time," was the second strategy Nutro employed. It was a very simplistic and rather modest approach compared to brands like Procter & Gamble, Colgate-Palmolive, and other large consumer packaged goods companies who used media such as TV as their main mode of marketing. Selling one bag at a time took the long way, and was certainly the "road less traveled." Nutro employees would have a conversation with one individual, during which they passionately shared all the benefits of feeding the product to their pets. It was a conversation that all Nutro's people, not just the sales team, used to genuinely connect and learn about someone's dog or cat, educate people on ingredients, and make a product recommendation to improve the life of that pet.

To be able to convert a customer was a badge of honor within the company. It created a competitive environment that encouraged the sales people to convert five people a day, a goal that was later changed to seven people a day. Salespeople interacted with everyone in the pet and feed stores.

Converting seven people a day might not seem *that* impactful. In the beginning, when the company employed just five salespeople, it was slow going. So they decided that for every 10 new trucks of pet food sold, they'd hire a new salesperson. "Sell more, hire more" soon became a tactic the team used to ramp up sales. Just 10 short years later, the sales team had gone from five people to 125, and in another 10, the team topped nearly 350 people.

The reason was again simple: sell the food on the store shelf to the consumer; the retailer then needs to reorder; the distributor has to reorder to fill their *own* pipeline; and sales generate exponentially. In 1976, there was one remarkable salesperson: Ed Brown. Some people imagine the typical salesperson as the fast-talking, dishonest used car seller, whose primary aim is to get the sale, not help the customer get what they need. Ed could not have been more different from this stereotype. He had an uncanny ability to remember a storeowner's name, along with all their employee's names and pertinent information about what was going on in each of their lives. Ed made people feel as if they were of the utmost importance. He could make a connection with anyone, and before long, he was preaching the gospel of chicken, rice, and lamb.

Ed believed in the power of conversion, a critical outlook as the one and only sales person in 1976. He drove around the West Coast in his Celebrity station wagon, traveling from San Diego up through Los

Angeles and into San Francisco, where he sold storeowners on the importance of offering Nutro in their stores. Twenty-five years later, one sales person explained it this way: "Conversion was the strategy, but it unfolded in an amazing way. Committing to [converting] five people per day to Nutro . . . forced us to be in the stores telling the story, and we were good at what we did. The interesting side effect was that we were there to capture every opportunity and tied up so much of the retailer's money into our displays and expansions that it left them with little left to put behind other brands. They had to sell *us* to make room for the next display . . . But guess who was there selling the next display? We were. Conversion became floor space, shelf space, and retail domination. You can't sell competitive product if you don't have the money to buy it or space to sell it."

With more true conversions, consumers readily bought the product and became loyal customers who would then tell others about Nutro. Once a consumer who had an itchy dog fed Nutro and saw a glossier skin and coat and a happier, more comfortable dog, they became a customer for the life of that pet. This became the power of conversion, which translated into the next strategy: gaining recommendation.

9

Belly-to-Belly Strategy #3: Recommendation Is King

"People often say that motivation doesn't last. Well, neither does bathing. That's why we recommend it daily."
—Zig Ziglar

Gaining recommendation was a daily, if not by-the-minute, ritual that involved several demographics. First, it meant having a conversation with consumers that involved a variety of questions, normally starting with "Do you have a dog or a cat?" Which usually followed with, "What is your dog's name?" The conversation continued to engage the pet parent until the sales person could make a recommendation.

Loyal consumers who fed the product to their pets and told others about their positive experience added to this recommendation process, thereby selling these additional pet owners on the concept and food. Having recommenders helped increase sales. Recommenders also came from the store staff whom consumers asked, "What food should I feed my dog or cat?" or "What food do you feed?" The desired response was Nutro.

Retailers had great reasons to recommend the food. Often, store employees were rewarded or thanked for these efforts and received free food to feed their own animals. Back in the 80s, the average federal minimum wage[21] for a retail employee was $3.35, and a 40-pound bag of Nutro Natural Choice was $24.99. It would therefore take an hourly employee nearly eight hours or one full workday to pay for this bag. The company realized this discrepancy and wanted to thank those recommenders with a free bag of food and acknowledge that the recommender would continue to advocate Nutro to new consumers.

On the last day of one national sales meeting, the character known as "Father Dewey" conducted his first appearance—or rather, skit—based on the importance of gaining recommendation. Father Dewey was playfully dressed in a collarino, a black dress shirt with a white tab collar commonly used by clergy. He proceeded to give his first "sermon" on the gospel of chicken, rice, and lamb, which became known as the Ten Nutro Consumer Commandments (see appendix). The room filled with roaring laughter and probably a bit of bewilderment from some who were a little taken aback by the skit's religious theme.

However, everyone stood as we all recited the Ten Consumer Commandments, which further showed the alliance we all had to ensure we had the retailer's best interest. We were all then served a thimble-size cup of apple juice to toast to our commitment in living the Ten Consumer Commandments.

---

21. http://www.infoplease.com/ipa/A0774473.html

1. Thou shalt know thy product and its benefits and why it is different.
2. Empathize with the customer. Help them understand how Nutro products can solve their problems.
3. Be organized and efficient—time is precious.
4. Be prompt—quick response earns respect.
5. Follow through; build loyalty.
6. Provide solutions. Anyone can define a problem. Successful people provide solutions.
7. Be on time. Don't miss your opportunity.
8. Work hard. Keep your customers satisfied.
9. Be enthusiastic. It is contagious.
10. Be honest.

Recommendation helped all sales people in the organization increase their sales. An employee who had a "Nutro store," meaning that everyone in the store was a Nutro recommender, secured some serious bragging rights. These stores were worth their weight in gold; each of them was highly valued and contributed to the company's overall success. These Nutro stores contributed to the fast and continued growth, and were truly the keys to the kingdom of Nutro's success. Even the competition knew it. Salespeople considered any attempt by a competitor to overtake one of these stores to be a personal affront, and the competitor could expect to feel the heat come back tenfold.

10

Belly-to-Belly Strategy #4: People

"If you want one year of prosperity, grow grain.
If you want ten years of prosperity, grow trees.
If you want 100 years of prosperity, grow people."
—Chinese Proverb

People were the conduit to all things at Nutro. Every piece of information traveled by and through people, no matter what team you worked on. And Nutro made a conscious choice to use the word *team* rather than department to illustrate the connectedness of Nutro's people and emphasize how they worked so seamlessly together.

In his book *Good to Great*, author Jim Collins discusses having the "right people in the right seat on the bus." While I have always loved this quote and refer to it frequently, I came upon an article Collins wrote called "Hitting the Limits: Realizing That Vertical Limits Aren't."[22] In it, Collins refers to an article written by James Logan

---

22. http://www.jimcollins.com/article_topics/articles/hitting-the-wall.html#articletop

called "Mount Robson's Emperor Face"[23] in which Logan recounts his third attempt and successful 1978 summit on the legendary Emperor Face Mountain with his climbing partner, Mugs Stump. Together, Mugs and James had decided they would climb the highest peak in the Canadian Rockies, a summit topping 12,994 feet. Collins makes the point when telling this story that it is not the "what" of the strategy that is important; it's *who* you are doing it with. The person James took with him to face this challenge was what helped him reach the top.

Similarly, Dave Traitel and Ed Brown scaled the mountain of pet food together. Each brought a set of strengths to the organization and capitalized on those strengths. As discussed previously, people have described Dave as a visionary with excellent business acumen, much like Steve Jobs. Those around him saw Dave as a genuine leader, a man of the utmost honesty and integrity. He was a truth-seeker, someone who knew the company's numbers extremely well and had a gut instinct to make the right financial decisions. Despite this intuition, Dave always sought others' opinions and always remained open to hearing the other person's side when debating an issue. He took risks, was willing to go the distance and play ball against "the big guys," and he *won*, time and time again.

Together, Dave and Ed demonstrated the importance of deciding, "Who are we going to do this with?" when undertaking a significant endeavor. They employed a team of amazing people over the years (all of whom are noted in this book's dedication).

As this once-small southern California company headed north, east, and across borders, it grew its human capital to be the best team in

23. http://publications.americanalpineclub.org/articles/12197912200/print

the pet food industry. To enjoy this kind of success, Nutro's people spanned a variety of roles and functions, and all played an essential part in building this remarkable organization.

Sales and Marketing

Some organizations are marketing-led organizations supported by sales. However, Nutro was just the opposite and everyone knew it. It was a sales-driven company and supported by marketing. What the sales people wanted, the sales people got, and the people in these two roles worked hand-in-hand.

As the company grew, sales people who did well were promoted to sales managers; sales managers who did well were then promoted to marketing. The sales team communicated frequently and passionately what they were hearing and seeing out in the field to the marketing team. In turn, the marketing team worked relentlessly and passionately to create programs, promotions, and products in record time.

In fact, they completed many product introductions within 90 days, going from inception to design, formulation, marketing, packaging, and manufacturing in just three months. According to some marketing gurus, this process can often take anywhere from 18 months to three years or longer. The interconnectedness of Nutro's team is what allowed employees to use the free flow of information to seal their competitive advantage.

Executive Level

Seeing the big picture and creating the vision for the future was what the executive leadership prepared for. A decade before owner Dave

Traitel sold the company, he allowed the then-president to begin interviewing other future presidents. He knew that Nutro needed a succession plan. If *you* owned an independently owned and operated family business and no one in the family wanted to run or was qualified to operate that business in coming years, what would *you* do? Odds are that you would sell it. So the vision was to hire a new co-president that would slowly integrate into the organization, take the helm, and financially prepare it for its eventual sale. This turned out to be nearly a 10-year plan to finalize.

Dave frequently let people at Nutro's national sales meetings know that he always had some offer on the table from some company or person wanting to purchase. During one period in the late 90s, rumors were running rampant about a possible purchase. Dave announced at a sales meeting, "Yes, some of you may have heard we were approached, and as of right now we are not selling to Mars—the company or the planet." Dave was proud to be Nutro's sole proprietor.

Distributors

The strategy of putting people first went beyond the boundary of Nutro's employees. Nutro sought to partner with individuals and organizations they perceived to be the best distributors. One might assume this meant that distributors received the utmost respect, kindness, and caring; unfortunately, this was not the always the case. Often, both parties experienced a Nutro-distributor partnership that was somewhat adversarial.

The company viewed some distributors as a credit and delivery mechanism for the product; as a result, some felt used and abused at the close of every month. One general manager of a distributor described his experience with Nutro as "holding our distributorship over our heads. We were threatened with the possibility of not being a Nutro distributor if we did not make our monthly number. And it felt like a regular occurrence." Yet if you asked these very same distributors who were the hardest-working, most dedicated sales team, they would tell you it was team Nutro every time.

The "With Whom" Connection

Everyone in the organization was passionate about the product they sold. Each person truly believed that Nutro was bulletproof. If someone did not hold this belief, he or she likely didn't work at Nutro for long. The company was a family that spanned 50 states and over 26 countries and sold on six of the seven continents. (I doubt any had distribution in Antarctica!)

We greeted each other warmly with a hug at meetings. The company was small enough for all employees to know each other well. As a team member fondly described, "We shared stories about successes at work and celebrated successes at home and with our families. I knew every one of my co-workers' families from their spouses to their kids. We grew more to love each other in friendship than simply as co-workers. This is [especially] interesting because I never had a co-worker who lived less than 120 miles from me. [But] distance was no issue . . . we lived with one another, fought with one another, and loved one another."

One colleague suggested that the law of attraction was at play at Nutro, meaning that people simply attract whatever they think about, positive or negative. Most folks at Nutro were like-minded and constantly heard that they were absolutely the best in the business. In fact, the mantra the "World's Best Pet Food" was something that everyone always shared when telling the Nutro story and converting a new consumer. Each person lived and breathed this mantra with every fiber in their being, and as one team member explained, "But it was the people who made the company so worthwhile. So many dedicated workers. We all believed in the product and the philosophy."

The following poem, "What Will Matter," written by Michael Josephson in 2003, is an example of not what we had to do, but rather what we gave to each other:

> Ready or not, some day it will all come to an end.
> There will be no more sunrises, no minutes, hours or days.
> All the things you collected, whether treasured or forgotten
> will pass to someone else.
> Your wealth, fame and temporal power will shrivel to irrelevance.
> It will not matter what you owned or what you were owed.
> Your grudges, resentments, frustrations
> and jealousies will finally disappear. So too, your hopes,
> ambitions, plans and to-do lists will expire.
> The wins and losses that once seemed so important will
> fade away.
> It won't matter where you came from
> or what side of the tracks you lived on at the end.
> It won't matter whether you were beautiful or brilliant.
> Even your gender and skin color will be irrelevant.
>
> So what will matter?
> How will the value of your days be measured?
>
> What will matter is not what you bought
> but what you built, not what you got but what you gave.

> What will matter is not your success
> but your significance.
>
> What will matter is not what you learned
> but what you taught.
> What will matter is every act of integrity,
> compassion, courage, or sacrifice
> that enriched, empowered or encouraged others
> to emulate your example.
>
> What will matter is not your competence
> but your character.
> What will matter is not how many people you knew,
> but how many will feel a lasting loss when you're gone.
> What will matter is not your memories
> but the memories that live in those who loved you.
> What will matter is how long you will be remembered,
> by whom and for what.
>
> Living a life that matters doesn't happen by accident.
> It's not a matter of circumstance but of choice.
> Choose to live a life that matters.

Working in this organization certainly did consume a lot of time, yet people generously gave this time to a cause they believed in. Therefore, it did not seem like work for many employees. As one past employee recounted, "Working at Nutro didn't feel like a job; the relationships that were created will never be forgotten."

One past president emphasized, "It is equally important to note that the *consistency* of the strategy was a strategy as well," like any team who practices their plays over and over again.

Vince Lombardi, who many consider the world's best football coach in history, said to his teams: "The difference between a successful person and others is not a lack of strength, not a lack of knowledge, but rather a lack of will."

Nutro's belief in and execution on these four key strategies showed that consistency and perseverance can get a company very far.

11

Creating Camelot: The Nutro Culture

> ***"Customers will never love a company until the employees love it first."***
> —*Simon Sinek*

We've all heard the saying "Which came first: the chicken or the egg?" The Nutro equivalent of this question was "Which came first: the product or the people?"

We know the company founders' intention was to create a corporate design that contained a "self-regeneration potential," so we believe that the people came first. Nutro's employees served as the nucleus of the organization. These team members were central to the creation of everything, and the senior leadership team knew it, as they helped shape it.

People who worked at Nutro went so far as to describe the culture and the way that all team members felt about both the company and each other as "Camelot." Some people may not be familiar with the legend of Camelot, a mystical city known to represent a magical place in time, where all members of its community shared the same passion and purpose. Camelot is a place where people come together to celebrate everything in its goodness and where the impossible is made possible. It's the perfect blend of harmony and good will, and you know that you have been there because *you have felt this experience firsthand.*

There are a few other words that we feel describe the uniqueness of Nutro's culture. Mojo is one, defined by Merriam-Webster as "a power that may seem magical and that allows someone to be very effective, successful, etc." Marshall Goldsmith[24] said this on mojo: "Mojo is the moment when we do something that's purposeful, powerful, and positive and the rest of the world recognizes it."

So what is "*it*?" Some, like psychologist Mihaly Csikszentmihalyi, call it "flow"—the "effortless action [people] feel in moments that stand out as the best in their lives."[25] For us, the culture that Nutro created produced a competitive advantage for the organization and enabled people to move mountains. As demand increased, the little giant moved eastward to serve more consumers. To say the culture was simply positive psychology that capitalized on the human spirit and brought to life creativity, intrinsic motivation, and optimism does not fully explain Nutro's "mojo." It was more than that.

According to psychologist Edgar Schein (1994), culture is based on three principles: (1) artifacts, or observable actions within a group; (2) understanding and embracing the values, beliefs, and goals in place; and (3) fully understanding and embracing the nature of

24. Goldsmith, Marshall. *Mojo: How to Get It, How to Keep It, How to Get It Back If You Lose It* (Grand Central Publishing, 2010).

25. https://www.psychologytoday.com/articles/199707/finding-flow

relationships, even as they apply to time and nature. Schein also provided a formal definition of culture: "A pattern of shared basic assumptions that the group learned as it solved its problems of external adaptation and internal integration that has worked well enough to be considered valid and, therefore, to be taught to new members as the correct way to perceive, think, and feel in relation to those problems." (p. 12)

In layman's terms, culture is "how we do things around here." The three principles from Schein help us to unravel this mystery of the Nutro culture and how its members made that magic happen.

Artifacts and Actions

Artifacts include everything we see about the company—the rituals, lingo, symbols, and even how people dress. The Nutro culture was able to create a powerful impact using symbols, one of which we see in Figure 16.

Figure 16: Photo of Japanese manufacturer in Tokyo
Source: Christie Cooper.

This photo, taken of a Japanese pet food manufacturer in Tokyo, shows how one culture can influence another. Japan has an elaborate code for etiquette. When I traveled to Japan to work with this team, I'd been warned that a training class there would not be the same as in the United States. I was told to prepare for no questions and blank stares. Yet this photo clearly depicts an interaction that has relaxed into something like a skit from *Saturday Night Live* and gives new meaning to Steve Martin's claim: "I'm a wild and crazy guy!"

It was critical for Nutro to convey their most valued strategy: product ingredient differential. They did this by calling on "the power of the chicken." Employees used a rubber chicken containing guts made of yarn to show the differential. It might sound a little hokey, but Nutro put chicken meal on the map of success. As discussed in the previous chapter, while Procter & Gamble, Colgate-Palmolive, Nestle, and Purina were using by-products, Nutro made sure the consumer saw the *value* of chicken meal, an ingredient with a premium price. In fact, it was essentially the same chicken that consumers purchased in the grocery store to put on the dinner table for their families, just with the water and fat removed. Cost was not a consideration at Nutro. Using pricier ingredients and their formulation contributed to the products' value and ultimate success.

The rubber chicken was a marketing item the sales team could order just like they could order brochures. A Nutro manager who gave his or her sales team a recipe for success might provide something like this:

Recipe: Gain Recommendation

Ingredients:

- ☐ 1 rubber chicken
- ☐ 1 pair of scissors and safety razor
- ☐ 1 dog food bowl
- ☐ 1 trash can
- ☐ Bic lighter
- ☐ 3 feet of laundry dryer duct about 6-8 inches in diameter
- ☐ Miniature chicken on a key chain

Instructions:

1. In front of a comfortably seated audience, sitting upon stacks of dog food displays or a 50-pound container of cat litter, begin using your props to engage the audience. First, ask them what they feed their dog or cat. Make a mental note most are feeding something with by-products in it. Ask the audience if they found a food with better ingredients, would they feed it to their pets? The answer is always yes (unless someone is a jokester).
2. Next, place dog food bowl on the tabletop or object for all to see. Pick up rubber chicken and ask for a volunteer. Hand scissors to volunteer and ask them to cut off chicken head and chicken feet. Have a volunteer discard "these ingredients" next to dog food bowl. Next, have them pick up safety razor and make an incision on belly of rubber chicken. Then, have them remove innards or guts from chicken (the yarn) and place next to other parts of chicken.

The main point to make is this: the heads, feet and guts are used in by-products. Would you feed this to your family? The answer is always no, and a mixture of other emphatically used words to indicate how gross this is. Next, place remaining chicken body in the dog food bowl. This is fresh chicken. Which would you rather feed your family? How about your pet?

Thank the current volunteer and have them sit down. Ask for two new volunteers. Have each hold up an end of the dryer duct. Have volunteer place the chicken body inside the dryer duct. Using the Bic lighter, flick the flame on under the dryer duct as if you were cooking the chicken. Take a miniature chicken on a key chain out of your pocket discretely and have volunteer B act is if they are taking out the chicken from the dryer duct. Say, "It went in as chicken and weighed more. Since that chicken was cooked, it cooked out the water and fat, and the end product was much smaller in size and weight." State emphatically, "It takes five pounds of fresh chicken to make one pound of chicken meal." Ask the audience: "What is the key take-away? There is more chicken in chicken meal than in fresh, whole chicken!"

This exercise was just one of many used to tell the story about the "differential." Employees used this play out of the Nutro playbook repeatedly over the years as the company grew from nine salespeople in 1986, to 150 in 1996, to over 300 salespeople by the year 2004. Consistency became a part of the strategy.

The artifacts or props that employees utilized had increased from just rubber chickens and chicken on a key chain to chicken ties, chicken hats, white chicken lab coats, and even chicken necklaces (see Figure 17). Salespeople used these artifacts to help drive the messaging on the ingredient differential.

FIGURE 17: PHOTO OF JAPANESE MANUFACTURER IN TOKYO
Source: Christie Cooper.

The photo to the left was one we commonly took of Nutro seminar attendees. People wanted to belong to this group called Nutro, whose members brought infectious excitement and fun to others. One European sales person even named the wackiness of the Nutro culture "the Nutro virus." This individual showed up to a national sales meeting with stickers designed to look like a virus, which he rapidly distributed to everyone in the audience. Each audience member promptly placed the stickers on the name badge hanging around their neck. It was great to see our European counterparts so passionate about the products we were selling in the States.

The Nutro virus was infectious. Before long, it was spreading quickly and Nutro was growing sales—*fast.*

Values, Beliefs, and Goals

In 2016-17, we surveyed over 100 Nutro employees and asked them to use adjectives to describe the culture of the organization. From this list of words, we get a glimpse into the inner workings of an organization that created not just a community but also a family (Figure 18).

FAMILY HARD **FUN** COMPETITIVE **PASSIONATE**

Figure 18: Word cloud of adjectives used to describe the culture of Nutro

Fun

Most people don't automatically associate this word with their jobs, but having fun at work *is* important. Dr. David Abramis,[26] a researcher on methods of creating highly motivating work places, found that people who have fun at work are more productive, more creative, make better decisions, and get along better with their colleagues.

---

26. Abramis, D.J. (December 01, 1994). Work Role Ambiguity, Job Satisfaction, and Job Performance: Meta-Analyses and Review. *Psychological Reports,* 75, 1411-1433.

They're less likely to be late, and they have fewer absences—a win-win for both company and the employee.

While fun was not an outcome that Nutro's founders intentionally set out to create, it happened organically.

Employees experienced fun in a variety of ways, from wins at retail to the bi-annual sales meetings the company held. These meetings—Tahoe and Christmas—were one way that owner Dave Traitel used to inspire and thank his team and their families.

The Lake Tahoe meeting was held in June. The crisp, clear air and greenery were a refreshing break from the daily grind of selling the World's Best Pet Food. Getting to Tahoe after working the first five months of the year was a nice break, and from the sales team's perspective, the trip was even sweeter if they'd accomplished their sales goals throughout the year. May and November were historically the months with the highest sales goals and revenue generation. No one wanted to show up to a sales meeting having not made the months prior to the meeting. Whatever happened, the sales regions would have the grit and determination to bring home the number in these months.

Everyone in the company worked hard, and everyone played hard at Lake Tahoe. The owner provided an "outing allowance" to each employee, a small stipend to participate in any activity they wanted the day before the sales meeting. These activities ranged from going to the spa for a massage, hang gliding, boating, canoeing, hiking, renting dirt bikes, and others. It was the owner's way of saying "thank you for all you do" in a heartfelt way that employees appreciated. People participated in these activities with their teammates, which further strengthened team rapport and relationships.

"Work hard and play hard" was certainly a motto that many at Nutro believed in and celebrated. A lot of the opportunities to celebrate, talk shop, and catch up happened at Rookies, the local sports bar in South Shore Lake Tahoe. Usually, the Canadian team became most competitive in drinking games while playing foosball or billiards. Indeed, their fierce, almost warrior-like attitude came through in their substantial sales increases year over year.

One of the best IT support folks explained it as follows: "Nutro led the natural pet food industry, and the sales division led Nutro. What sales wanted, sales got. Marketing and R&D, sparsely populated departments, existed to serve the insatiable demands of one of the last feet-in-the-street selling machines. It was almost a cult, stuffed to the rafters as it were with high-octane, hard-drinking, road-warrior, half-crazy salesmen and women."

The Christmas meeting was truly a very special and memorable week. Spouses were invited to attend, and the company covered all travel costs. The trip gave employees' spouses the chance to see all the people their husband or wife worked with, and created closeness between both colleagues and families. Spouses attended a luncheon and a tour during the first day of the sales meeting, while employees participated in the meeting.

The highlight of the Christmas meeting was certainly the Christmas party. No expense was spared. Once the company became big enough, the Christmas party moved from the home of David and Joan Traitel to the Jonathan Club, a political club established in 1895 that had evolved into a social club. Up until nearly the late 1980s, this club's membership was men only. Women attending the

Nutro sales meeting had to be escorted by a male member around the facilities.

Eventually, company executives sought out another setting for the party, and ended up choosing the Ritz-Carlton in San Marino, California, as the new very nice, and very upscale Christmas meeting venue. Formal business attire was required, although a suit and tie seemed like overkill for this rather casual company and just did not seem to suit particular segments of the meeting, such as "How to Conduct a Seminar." People who were skilled in capturing audience participation were always a highlight of the meeting. These people would conduct a mini-seminar for the audience, which normally contained many a newbie.

One such skit seemed to be reminiscent of a Gallagher comedy act. Leo Gallagher was a comedian who was known for using props as a part of his act. In particular, he was very fond of using watermelons and whacking them open with a very large mallet. So one afternoon for the mini-seminar breakout session, a manager from the Midwest conducted a similar act using a watermelon and a mallet, and requiring the two front rows to wear inexpensive rain gear attire (actually, just a garbage bag with a hole cut out for a person's head).

Now remember, all of this was taking place at the *Ritz-Carlton*. The thick, plush, cream-colored carpeting was soon soaked with watermelon chunks, seeds, and juice, along with the drapes and the white tablecloths on the rectangular tables in front of each attendee. It was a mess. That was the last meeting we had at the Ritz, which probably wasn't a coincidence.

Either because we outgrew the Ritz (or weren't allowed to return), Palm Springs became the new home of the December national meeting. The surroundings were much more relaxed and casual, and therefore a much better fit with the company's culture.

Family

This was the second word used with the most frequency when describing the culture. The owner's generosity, and the way he made those in *his* organization feel like they were *his* family, was central to this. It is an instinct to want to take care of and defend your family, and Dave protected his flock. His generosity extended to even preparing and cooking the meat at the manufacturing plant company BBQ.

Dave knew everyone and acknowledged everyone. There are numerous stories of individuals who were facing tough personal issues, many of which surrounded medical conditions. Situations ranged from kidney transplants to alcohol abuse to funeral arrangements. Dave Traitel subsidized many of these situations.

One employee shared his gratitude and the following story: "Nutro was a company who truly cared about their people. During my tenure with Nutro, I was diagnosed with multiple sclerosis and was unable to work. I received nothing but compassion during this difficult time. I received calls from [my manager] checking in on me regularly and reassuring me that Nutro [would] always have a place for me, for as long as it [took]. [He only cared] about my well-being to support my recovery. Nutro continued to pay me to ensure that my family and I didn't suffer any further hardship. I truly believe that this played a vital role in my recovery and [allowed me to] return to work after three months. I will forever be grateful!"

Esprit de corps, a feeling of pride, fellowship, and common loyalty, was apparent at numerous events at national sales meetings. In particular, two were highly recognized events by survey respondents: the Annual Chili Cook-Off and the Pet Food Peddler.

FIGURE 19: ANNUAL CHILI COOK-OFF
PICTURED FROM LEFT TO RIGHT:
SCOTT KELLER, FRANK HON, GREG HUTSELL, AND DON CARLSON
Photo credit: Christie Cooper.

The Annual Chili Cook-Off was held in June during the Lake Tahoe national meeting. Each of the six regions created their own theme and made their booth a fun event. Regions generally assigned a small team to develop a concept or idea that would be the basis for all costumes or attire that each region's team would wear. The Southwest Region (Figure 19) went so far as to create a skit based on the movie *Wyatt Earp*. (You might notice the holstered guns on the hips of the individuals below. The hotel's security department was notified of the use of these child's guns as props.)

Each region turned in their chili recipe to Peggy Pennington, Dave Traitel's administrative assistant and the ultimate meeting planner. Peggy ensured that everyone received all the chili ingredients they needed. Each region elected a chef who picked others to help in the preparation. One region arranged an impromptu team meeting

FIGURE 20: ANNUAL CHILI COOK-OFF JUDGING
PICTURED FROM LEFT TO RIGHT:
DAVE KRAVIS, JERRY SICHERMAN, LADD HARDY, MIKE SATTERWHITE AND DAVE TRAITEL
Photo credit: Lori Thomas.

in advance of the Tahoe sales meeting to serve various chilis that were then voted on. The winning recipe was served to the judges at the Tahoe Chili Cook-Off (Figure 20).

Nutro made a competition out of everything, and the Chili Cook-Off was no different. Employees cherished this face-to-face time. As one employee shared, "I miss Nutro . . . miss Tahoe and Palm Springs, and I miss the friendships. I keep connected via Facebook and LinkedIn, but there was just something about those semi-annual sales meetings. Serious bonding went on there. They were like family reunions."

Passionate

The feeling of family was prevalent everywhere, and was so strong that no matter where someone was, they wanted to be sure that consumers had the opportunity to belong to this family by feeding their pets the product. Competitors saw this as a "cult." Those inside the company knew others were saying this, but it was more than okay with them; it was a really a badge of honor, according to one employee: "Nutro was a family and became part of your identity. In addition to [encouraging] personal goal setting, it created an intense team-based program that held you accountable [to both yourself and to others]. We created a cult-like phenomenon behind an industry-leading product."

For those who worked *inside* the company, the word passionate came up very frequently, so much so that some might see it as cult-like. But it simply conveyed an intense love of the product and the view that any other product was inferior. Nutro team members went to great lengths to share this love they had for the products they sold.

Passion extended beyond the product; people were passionate about *each other*. Team members felt an incredible sense of camaraderie: "[There was an] environment of internal competition along with feeling like a band of brothers and sisters, coupled with an incredible selling story that, at the time, competitors could not rival. And somehow, [Nutro had] the ability to find the most amazing people to work with in the industry. They were not just bodies with order pads and a set of car keys. They were, and still are . . . the gold standard of associates. The truly passionate amongst us, no matter when they became part of the Nutro family, treated the brand as if it were their own child. We were passionate about the brand and knew that its success reflected directly on ourselves and our success."

As another leader told it, "[Nutro was] an energetic and confident company with a passion and drive rarely seen. Great people, all of whom were incredibly charismatic and [also] great *leaders* of people."

Everyone who worked at the company displayed an entrepreneurial spirit. Plenty of people said that being a salesperson at Nutro was the next closest thing to owning your own business. Each salesperson treated their territory as if it *was* truly their business.

Competitive

Nutro created and delivered rewards in a way that encouraged competition. The friendly rivalry started out among only a few individuals in the early days. Later on, when the company had six regions across the U.S. and Canada, competition became much fiercer. Everyone who worked at Nutro had an incredible will to win, succeed, and never give up.

This desire for success transcended many individuals' personal lives. One particular employee commented, "Our goal was not simply to sell dog food, but to convert the minds and hearts of every consumer, retail associate, buyer, family member, and so on. We loved to be hated by every competitor. Gunslingers deal in lead; we dealt in kibble and there wasn't another company around who could put us down. We were the outlaw and the sheriff, and we owned not just main street but the whole town."

Regardless of the department, each team member certainly had a sense of pride.

Hard Work

Anyone in the pet industry would likely agree that Nutro employed the hardest-working individuals between 1975 and 2007. If an employee did not exemplify hard work, they did not last long. Management expected their teams to put in long hours. In doing this, some might say that Nutro employees made a great sacrifice by being away from their families to achieve the company's goals.

However, this hard work was not something that Nutro workers saw as a sacrifice, since everyone on the team, even down to the warehouse workers, received a bonus. Everyone loved or at least cared deeply for one another. As mentioned previously, most felt that working at Nutro was the closest thing to owning their own businesses. We gave our sweat, heart, and tears to make the company successful.

When the competitors ended their day, many Nutro employees would still be out at their retail stores selling promotions, setting up a display, or educating store employees after hours. We didn't have to be told to do this; we just did it.

As one salesperson explained, the competition wanted to be like Nutro: "The feeling of family and enthusiasm for making and selling the world's best dog food we had during our sales meetings, and the competitive spirit we had during the early days of the pet food peddler competition . . . these are two things that pet companies today try to emulate."

Nature of Relationships

Relationships, between both internal and external customers, were vital to the organization's success. There were certainly personality conflicts from time to time, and of course, egos did get in the way occasionally, as is bound to happen at any company. But most people enjoyed who they worked for *and* with. It's an amazing thing to be able to go to work and love what you do. Working on a team of people with whom you have such a strong bond makes for an even more incredible experience.

The competition tried hard to mimic what Nutro was doing out in the field with retailers and consumers, and I suppose that would be the best form of flattery. However, it was a difficult task for the competition to actually *complete* what we did themselves.

Some organizations out there today, such as Disneyland and Zappos, offer "university"-type training. In essence, individuals and companies can go to Zappos to learn what makes their culture and customer service unique. For about $6,000, people can sign up for the Zappos Culture Camp and learn about things like core values, on-boarding new employees, creating employee engagement and happiness, and hiring for a culture fit. And if you don't care to spend that much money, you can at least check out their culture book.[27] The culture at Zappos is the closest we have seen to our experience at Nutro. They begin with clearly stated values and goals. Their team works hard together to achieve these goals, and then celebrates together as well.

Celebrations are another critical component to creating this kind of desired culture. Celebrating success can be a challenge in today's global landscape with remote work teams, but that's no reason to omit this essential step. Reveling in success and wins guarantees that your teams will become closer. This small investment can have rather large dividends. And it's helpful to have a reminder or memento of these celebrations!

One former Nutro employee explained, "I still carry the Nutro keychain I received in my first meeting 25-plus years ago. Ed Brown and this company gave me an opportunity of a lifetime that took me to places and exposed me to things I would never have done on my own without their spark, opportunity, and culture that prepared me for the battle ahead. Through it all, it was the time of my life and my career."

Nutro taught us and countless other employees the importance of creating and acting upon winning strategies for culture. While each company has its own degree of formality (or lack of it), consider how important the following elements are when building your own winning culture:

1. Create a simple vision that the people in the organization can understand and rally behind. This allows them to be truly passionate about the cause a company is working

---

27. https://www.amazon.com/2010-CULTURE-BOOK-Paperback-Zappos/dp/0615413269/

toward. For Nutro, it was simple: "Sell the world's best pet food, one bag at a time."

2. Encourage an entrepreneurial spirit. People want freedom and autonomy. When is the last time you heard someone say, "I'd prefer to be micromanaged"? Give people the tools to do their job and then get out of their way. Empowerment is an effective tool; use it. For the Nutro employees and in particular the sales team, it was the closest thing to owning their own businesses, and they treated it that way.
3. Keep in mind that there is no replacement for hard work, which at times can translate into long hours. But it can also translate into finding new processes and work streams to get the work done more efficiently. Hard work is also an attitude that does not stop until the person involved in the endeavor obtains his or her goal.
4. Remember the "with whom" syndrome. Just like Mugs Stump, who we talked about in chapter 9, taking a journey with someone whom you can really depend on is critical. Being able to love your job is one aspect; being able to call those you work with family is what creates a tight-knit team. This teamwork then becomes a competitive advantage. It is a model that organizations can pay to learn about, yet the process of carrying it out is entirely different. We'll look more closely at how Nutro did this in the next chapter.

12

Catalysts to Success: The Product

"Success is walking from failure to failure with no loss of enthusiasm."
—Winston Churchill

Numerous small wins contributed to Nutro's success; however, this chapter will focus on what we call the Big 5, which covers two main aspects: product and people. In this chapter, we will discuss product: specifically, the two main product launches that moved the company toward prominence. Chapter 13 will discuss the people: specifically, the three components that made Nutro's people such a critical part of the company's success.

We used qualitative research in the form of online surveys and in-person interviews as a way to collect data from all teams within the organization: manufacturing, operations, sales, marketing, administration, human resources, R&D, and accounting.

Each of the product catalysts we'll discuss allowed the company to continue to follow their goal to "sell one bag at a time" and improve the lives of pets. The areas of greatest success involved product creation, building a team, and retailer support. Let's look at each of these in detail.

Product Creation: Max

In 1985, after several unsuccessful attempts to create a new product called Max Stress, Sharon Machlik, whom we first introduced in chapter 6, joined the team at Nutro. Sharon had originally been hired to make a cat food line. However, Max Stress had been not finding success with its formulation, so Sharon transitioned to reformulate and reinvigorate the dog food line. In doing so, Max Stress was renamed simply Max.

Max's unique approach was to use an innovative blend of chicken, rice, and lamb. Dr. Machlik collaborated with Dr. Peter Ihrke, a veterinarian from U.C. Davis, whose expertise in companion animal dermatology is unmatched and highly regarded. While we don't have all the specifics of this working relationship, we do know that Dr. Ihrke had a significant impact on Dr. Machlik's ability to impart successful recipes that created pet foods formulated for a healthy skin and coat. In fact, Nutro patented this "formulated for healthy skin and coat" claim, along with the exact formulation. This claim gave credence to Max and subsequent Nutro foods. Dr. Machlik helped contribute to ensuring the food was "bulletproof" for the team steadfastly selling the products.

Product Creation: Natural Choice Lamb and Rice

In the late 1980s, the innovation from Nature's Recipe in creating a lamb formula roused the sales team at Nutro. An important debate was taking place within the company. Nature's Recipe was gaining shelf space, and sales grew steadily for them in a new category of pet food: lamb and rice.

Sales wanted the product; but marketing was skeptical, and select members of the executive team were strongly opposed to creating a product in this new category. Max dog food was gaining success, and Nutro employees were concerned that they would cannibalize their own sales. Months passed without an agreement. After much continued debate, many promising conversations flourished, and finally, in 1991, the internal teams reached a consensus to formulate Natural Choice Lamb and Rice.

The product gained instant success. Timing could not have been better, as Nutro had one edge over Nature's Recipe now: Natural Choice was formulated with rice, and Nature's Recipe used wheat. This made all the difference.

Nutro continued to gain momentum, while sales for Nature's Recipe soon came to a dead stop. Nature's Recipe became plagued with a vomitoxin contaminant, a substance found in wet grain that occurs while food is being transported by rail car across the country. However, companies that conduct in-house ingredient testing can easily detect vomitoxins and other health hazards for pets. But something went awry for Nature's Recipe, and a massive recall during the mid-90s forced them to take all their product off the shelves. It was surprising that they were able to rebound at all after this.

The Nutro sales team took full advantage of the Nature's Recipe faux pas. They were able to gain new placement of Natural Choice Lamb and Rice, since stores needed something to replace the faulty Nature's Recipe product. Soon, Natural Choice Lamb and Rice became the company's cash cow.

13

Catalysts to Success: Taking a New Initiative

"Risk comes from not knowing what you're doing."
—*Warren Buffett*

Three particular elements contributed most potently to the organization's acceleration: the demo team as well as leaving and then returning to the giant known as PetSmart.

Building a Demo Team

The purpose of this tactic was to educate, promote, and convert consumers who were using other pet food products. Nutro was the first to develop such a unique marketing strategy in the pet industry. The demo program started in 1982, with less than 15 demonstrators throughout Southern California. The goal was to reach as many consumers as possible who came through the front door of pet specialty stores, including military exchanges, commissaries, and various consumer shows. A demonstrator worked a shift, generally on the weekend, telling the Nutro story and trying to sell a bag of pet food to as many customers as possible.

Each sales person targeted the top 10 stores in their territory and tracked each one's progress. The goal was always to take our *unfair share,* a term used to denote the gain of market share, shelf space, and recommendation that Nutro seized from the competition. Ultimately, each account grew one bag and one consumer at a time.

Nutro did not have the funds the large conglomerates had to invest in television, magazines, large consumer booths, and free product offerings. Procter & Gamble, Colgate-Palmolive, Nestle, Purina, and Pedigree bought the lion's share of TV advertising that drove consumers to the pet stores. Then Nutro was present and ready in stores, happy to convert those consumers face-to-face.

Nutro was able to share their bulletproof story: "No Heads, No Feet, No Guts; Feed Less, Poop Less, and Shed Less." Each demonstrator was equipped with demo tables with the product precisely displayed. The demo team utilized the same props the sales team used while conducting their seminars: that infamous rubber chicken, along with chicken heads, feet, feces, and guts (yarn) in the dog bowl to represent to consumers the visual of what they might feed their dog(s). Charts that compared Nutro to as many as 10 other brands were on display to provide a visual aid for consumers showing the ingredients Nutro used versus their competitors.

Nutro demonstrators educated store workers, which empowered these staff members to recommend the products to new consumers seven days a week. The math was simple: convert 10 new customers a week, who then told 10 new people about the product, and the retailer would have hundreds of new customers in a matter of months, all the while ordering more pet food from the distributors.

As one Nutro employee emphasized, "Education was a big part of the marketing. The demo program was invaluable."

Initially, district managers (the outside salespeople) managed their demo staff and demo programs. They would pick the stores they wanted to grow in and hire the staff. Some district managers oversaw as many as 25-30 demonstrators in addition to their normal duties of selling, merchandising, and educating all the retailers in their own territory. Much was expected of the sales team, which required hard work and many more hours than the competitors most likely worked.

As Nutro grew, company leaders truly came to appreciate the importance of the demo program and its growth potential. They decided to hire staff specifically to oversee the demonstrators and give some relief to the district managers (DMs). This allowed the DMs to spend more time selling the product to the stores; in turn, the demo team would push the product out the front door.

Not surprisingly, the big conglomerates did not like Nutro. As the company gained a positive reputation via word of mouth and sales started to grow, competitors felt the strain on their sales. But Nutro was unstoppable. The demonstrators were well trained and continued to hold monthly demo meetings. The demonstrators' line managers would go out and work with them in the field to assist with any issues or difficulties they faced in converting consumers. And district managers would assist in field training as well. In fact, many DMs were a large source of motivation and inspiration for the demonstrators. As shown in the following photo, trying to make the

FIGURE 21: PICTURED FROM LEFT TO RIGHT: UNNAMED PETSMART STORE MANAGER; AARON SCHMIDT, DEMO MANAGER; UNNAMED PETSMART STORE MANAGER; LIA RIVADENEYRA, DM
Photo credit: Christie Cooper.

job fun was an important aspect for them (Figure 21).

Nutro's demo program became the example for other companies. Yet no matter how hard the competition tried to mimic this element of Nutro's success, they were never able to do it as well as Nutro. In fact, other pet food companies feared the program so much they tried many different ways to stop Nutro's approach—the most prevalent form being lawsuits.

Soon, Nutro found itself constantly defending the program and their demo team. Too frequently, David Traitel's little company was locked in a heated battle between Colgate-Palmolive and Procter & Gamble. But Traitel did not care if he spent more money in attorney's fees than the settlement he had expected to win just to make sure he won and the big guys lost.

Demonstrators commonly educated consumers by comparing ingredients and products. They taught store staff, vets, dog trainers, and new pet owners. Nutro trained pet parents how to read the labels of the product they were feeding their pets, and how to compare the ingredients, feeding levels, amount of waste, and skin and coat results. The most important advice demonstrators gave was specific directions on how to make the switch in a way that would help prevent pets from experiencing temporary digestive upset.

Nutro's demo program launched in the early 1980s and with just a handful of demo staff. By the beginning of 1993, three full-time territory demo managers (TDMs) wrote manuals on hiring, training, scheduling, and ongoing issues with the new and growing demo program. This documentation was carefully created to assist future employees in following the recipe for success. Later on, the company hired a TDM for each state, each of whom was responsible for hundreds of demo staff. By 2007, Nutro had over 3,500 part-time demonstrators converting and selling their products consistently across the United States, Canada, and Europe.

The company was always pushing the envelope to educate as many customers as possible on the product's many benefits. The distinction that Nutro offered to consumers and products met the age, weight, large breed, small breed, allergy prone pets, and grain-free needs, and of course, pets with skin and coat issues.

Nutro taught their demonstrators to be bold in approaching customers; you could often find them roaming the store and walking competitors' aisles with the mission to start a conversation. Nutro's demo team took pet food nutrition to a new level by learning as much as they could about the competitions' products.

The TDMs would conduct monthly demo meetings to highlight top accounts and top demo staff and to discuss what the team could do better to gain more new consumers and sales. The demonstrators felt appreciated, supported, and empowered; they were entrepreneurs of their program. They knew growth was occurring in stores because of *their* hard work, high conversions, and sales.

Nutro began using demonstrators at dog, cat, and consumer shows if the DM was unable to attend. The demo team members served as the voice of the customers; they were able to see what was going on in the marketplace and report on it. Pet shows were yet another spot for a wealth of information on what consumers were looking for. Demonstrators soon learned about what ingredients consumers wanted and did not want and pushed this information up through the company's top tiers. Nutro created many new items based on the feedback that demonstrators gathered directly from customers.

The demo team learned about upcoming promotions, product launches, and other intel that store managers were happy to share with their beloved Nutro demonstrator. As such, Nutro received firsthand information on the competitors' marketing and promotional calendar. The store staff saw the Nutro demonstrator as part of *their* store team, and therefore volunteered information on competitors' new product launches, product failures, and ingredient changes early.

This positive word of mouth went beyond just store employees. Dog groomers recommended the product to the hundreds of clients they saw monthly. The demo team gave dog trainers free samples of pet food and treats to pass out to their clients. One bag at a time and one consumer conversion at a time equaled thousands of bags a month of new growth as the fantastic team of demonstrators grew. Nutro's demo team was a well-oiled machine; retailers came to see their demonstrators as a great resource.

14

Catalysts to Success: Taking a Big Plunge

"The first step toward success is taken when you refuse to be a captive of the environment in which you first find yourself."
—Mark Caine

Retailer Support: Divorced From PetSmart

In 1995, after several years of partnering and conducting business with PetSmart, Nutro decided to dissolve their relationship with the pet mega-retailer. As of 2016, PetSmart had 1,466 locations in the United States, Canada, and Puerto Rico, and 53,000 store associates.

Back in 1992, the 50th PetSmart store had just opened in the United States.[28] At the time, Nutro felt that it was not receiving the support it needed from the large retailer. So after much consideration, Dave Traitel insisted that Nutro withdraw from their organization. At the time, PetSmart operated as more of a grocery store for pets.

---

28. https://corporateofficehq.com/petsmart-corporate-office/

There was little interaction between consumer and employee, which meant that PetSmart did not appreciate the benefit of Nutro's demo program or allow it to thrive. As a result, all ties between the organizations were severed.

The "divorce letter," dated May 29, 1995, read like this:

> Dear Mr. Parker,
>
> On a number of occasions during the past 12 months or so, representatives of our respective companies have discussed the substantial disagreements our two companies have over how Nutro's pet food products should be promoted in PetSmart's stores. Because these disagreements appear to be irreconcilable and involve matters of critical importance to Nutro, we have reluctantly concluded that Nutro has no alternative but to terminate its business relationship with PetSmart . . . As of July 1, 1992, Nutro will no longer honor any purchase orders from PetSmart . . . It is with considerable reluctance that Nutro takes this step to sever its relationship with PetSmart. However, PetSmart's philosophy as to how Nutro's products should be promoted in its stores is simply incompatible with Nutro's philosophy. I trust that each of us will cooperate with the other to ensure that the termination of our relationship may proceed in a spirit of good will and without conflict.
>
> Sincerely yours,
>
> David T. Traitel, President

A representative of PetSmart sent a fax with a sticky note over the letter from Mr. Traitel sharing the following:

> 7-17-95
>
> Dave,
>
> It's a lot of words that says [sic] nothing. Date conflict provides a glimpse of confusion at Nutro. Maybe our pets are better off without Nutro's products and philosophy . . .
>
> —Dudley . . .

This was a very bold move on Nutro's part. Company executives didn't feel that the direction in which PetSmart was going at the time—toward a warehouse club feel with a focus on low prices—was the direction in which Nutro was heading. Often, the megastore would sell the product for under cost and use "loss leaders" to gain traction. All the while, small, independently owned pet and feed stores were suffering the wrath of the then-discount giant.

Ironically, Nutro received a letter dated March 1, 1995, from Petco Senior Vice President of Merchandising and Distribution Larry Asselin, acknowledging Nutro.

> "Dear . . .,
>
> Allow me to take a moment to thank you for your support in making 1994 the most successful year in Petco history. As you know, our sales exceeded previous records and we know Nutro played a big part in this sales increase. Together, Petco and Nutro have built a large volume of business on the basis of product quality and competitive pricing and we are very proud of this reputation . . ."

So the team continued to focus on doing what it did best—selling one bag at a time—while supporting a new mantra: "No PetSmart." This refrain gained the still-growing pet food company much traction with independently owned pet specialty stores. As such, the sales team put all their focus and energy into this segment of the market. The team created tight-knit relationships with their customers and worked hard on their behalf to increase sales. Nutro's sales steadily grew while they continued to gain support and recommendation from retailers throughout the U.S. and globally.

Code Name Monica: Rebuilding a Partnership With PetSmart

Marketing consultant partner Annamarie Turano wrote this for the Retail Customer Experience group: "Price is not where PetSmart plays; lower prices can easily be found at Walmart, Target, and online specialty retailers. However, PetSmart's focus on trusted care minimizes the importance of price in the minds of pet owners."[29] This statement conveys the shift that the mega-retailer eventually made from low-cost leader to pet-parent supporter.

Government covert operations all seem to have secret code names, like the Acoustic Kitty, a CIA project from the 60s trying to use cats to spy on Soviet embassies, or the more famous Bay of Pigs, an unsuccessful invasion of Cuba. Well, Nutro had its own code name for going back to PetSmart. They called it "Monica."

You might wonder, "Why Monica?" Well, it was around the time that President Clinton was having inappropriate relations with an

29. http://www.retailcustomerexperience.com/blogs/how-smart-is-petsmart/

intern named Monica Lewinsky. Clandestine meetings were arranged between Nutro and PetSmart executives to begin discussions on entering back into a relationship. According to a Nutro marketing executive, "Both companies went so far as to check in with fictitious names, and we never stayed at the same hotel twice." Seems as though President Clinton and Nutro were both hiding relationships from the public.

By refocusing their goals and strategy, PetSmart regained Nutro's support, and the two companies strategically decided to "date" again. By 1999, Nutro received placement back on PetSmart's shelves. And by that time, those 50 stores had grown to over 500.[30] Nutro continued to revel in double-digit growth.

---

30. https://corporateofficehq.com/petsmart-corporate-office/

15

Lessons Learned: Dedicated to Entrepreneurs

> *"Never look back unless you are planning to go that way."*
> *—Henry David Thoreau*

I can still hear my mom telling me, "Sweetie, you need to learn from my mistakes. Don't make the same mistakes I did." Most kids don't care to hear this; after all, we think, *How much do our parents know?* However, the experiences from people who worked at Nutro can help other companies and entrepreneurs. These insights from individuals inside the company should serve as lessons learned from our mistakes.

So what *were* some of these mistakes?

Everyone Was a Zebra

In other words, everyone looked the same. The organization was very homogeneous and lacked diversity. Look at this classic picture, set in the 1960s (Figure 22). Compare it to the next photo (Figure 23), which shows a group of millennials enrolled at California State University involved in the Sales Leadership Center, earning a bachelor's degree along with a professional sales certificate. It is evident to see how diversity within organizations has changed over the last 60 years, bringing a wider variety of people together to share their ideas and expertise.

FIGURE 22: WWPSA MEETING; JOHN SALEEN IS PICTURED IN THE BACK ROW ON THE RIGHT
Unknown source.

FIGURE 23: CSUF SALES LEADERSHIP TEAM
Photo Credit: Mark Mantey, Co-Director of the Sales Leadership Center.

GENDER BIAS

This is another element that these two photos clearly depict. During the 60s, the workplace was still very much a place for men; they were the breadwinners, while women took care of the household. This type of cultural norm meant that organizations often overlooked women, didn't see them as equals, and therefore rejected them for senior-type management positions.

Up until May 2007, a female never held the role of president, vice president, or other C-suite positions at Nutro. While several women were an integral part of the business and certainly carried much clout, none received the appropriate or deserved C-suite title. This was not unusual in the 1970s and 80s; it was, unfortunately, the norm.

This pattern continued to pervade the organization. Some of the women and men we interviewed for this book shared their disappointment in the lack of diversity and inequality between males and females. One senior executive seemed to feel sincere remorse and shame over not hiring one particular female to run the manufacturing facility, especially since she was probably even more qualified than the male counterpart who interviewed for the same position.

Things were especially hard for working mothers. Bearing the burden (and joy) of child-rearing while juggling the demands of the job was quite difficult at times. Women at Nutro had to work just as hard and just as long as their male counterparts in order to be seen as successful, regardless of other demands in their lives. Whether male or female, demonstrating a robust work ethic, a drive for results, and a sense of resilience were all requirements to succeed.

There continues to be a great deal of debate regarding equal pay for men and women in the workplace, with questions about why women *still* don't earn as much as their male counterparts. Women's role as the primary caregiver in raising children might come into play here; there was certainly a concern at Nutro around women being able to do the same work a man could. If a woman took on a particular role, management worried she might become pregnant and then wondered how much she'd be able to work. This outlook ended up creating a very homogenous company comprised of mostly male, Caucasian employees between 30-50 years of age, with only slight variation.

A study conducted by McKinsey & Company found that women make up only about 14 percent of top executive committees in Fortune 500 companies, and very few CEOs[31] are female. Some individuals who

---

31. Barsh, Joanna, and Yee, Lareina. Unlocking the full potential of women at work (McKinsey & Company, 2012): https://www.mckinsey.com/capabilities/people-and-organizational-performance/our-insights/unlocking-the-full-potential-of-women-at-work

worked at Nutro expressed deep regret for potentially overlooking a woman for a role due to her gender.

Technology

Technology was never one of Nutro's strong suits. There's a well-known story from the mid-80s about the company's decision to purchase a fax machine. It was amazing how something seemingly so small could create such discussion! In the 70s and through the early 90s, fax machines and cell phones were nonexistent. The debate about increasing the company's technology resources grew and became rather heated. If material needed to get between departments, people, or others, employees frequently used Federal Express, without much thought to the costs. At some point, this caught up to employees, and the first corporate office fax machine was purchased (a thermal paper fax machine, no less!). Having a fax machine soon created "fax envy" among senior leaders and departments.

The organization wasn't much of a leader in other tech-related areas either. Most companies today consider technology to be something to "lean into." A study by MIT Sloan Management Review and Capgemini Consulting[32] found that "companies [having more than $1 billion in revenues] now face a digital imperative: adopt new technologies effectively or face competitive obsolescence."

This advice will likely prove instrumental for the pet industry as well, especially since e-commerce now represents one of the fastest growing segments in the pet channel. According to a Nielsen global

---

32. Fitzgerald, M. et al. Embracing Digital Technology (2013 Digital Transformation Global Executive Study and Research Project): https://sloanreview.mit.edu/projects/embracing-digital-technology/

pet food study (2015), e-commerce accounted for 2 percent of the global sales in 2013. The U.S. represented the largest of eight[33] countries leading this pace.

33. Nielsen Global Track Complete Sales Value and Industry Coverage Matrix

16

Memories

"Nothing is ever really lost to us as long as we remember it."
—L.M. Montgomery

Memories that previous team members have shared have been extremely helpful to us in writing this book. We're grateful to hear former Nutro employees' heartfelt insights and stories and have tried to the best of our ability to capture this feedback. People made all sorts of telling comments (in face-to-face interviews, phone interviews, or via an online survey) when describing their time at Nutro. We heard many sentiments like these:

- "The most fun and professionally rewarding time in my career."
- "An energetic and confident company with a passion and drive rarely seen. Great people, all of whom were incredibly charismatic and great leaders of individuals."
- "The most fantastic company you could ever work for!"

- "One of the best experiences of my life. I will never forget the time I worked here. It had a significant impact on my career."
- "High energy, demanding, fun, a once-in-a-life experience. I miss it . . . and everyone."
- "An intangible spirit permeated the Nutro sales force that drove us to new heights."
- "Fast-paced, hard work and we didn't know how good we were as a team. The likes will never be duplicated again in the pet industry, or others."
- "The best experience of my life and a real jolt into the very competitive pet trade."
- "A life-changing event in every way."

It's been a privilege to capture the hearts and minds of the team members who have worked for the company. Make no mistake: the company was not perfect; after all, no company is. However, many of us indeed experienced what we truly felt was a version of Camelot. For this, we all must thank our fearless leader, David Traitel (Figure 24).

FIGURE 24: NUTRO'S FEARLESS LEADER, DAVE TRAITEL
Photo Credit: Christie Cooper.

People use a variety of kind words to describe Dave: humble, genuine, and an authentic leader. He was a charming man of the utmost integrity. The honesty and morality he always displayed are competencies that are consistently in the top four of "must-haves" for a leader. Dave exuded these, and always sought the truth.

He managed to be a man of great strength and fortitude, yet at the same time, always very approachable. He believed in hiring the best people and then stayed out of their way and gave each person the autonomy to work in his company as if it was their business. One Nutro employee described it as "a true family-owned company where the owner valued his employees. The workers treated the company like it was [their] own business."

Dave was present at each national meeting, warmly greeting those entering and leaving the conference. A man of great generosity and selflessness, he sought to make the lives of pets better by providing the "best pet food in the world" and enriched the lives of those he employed as well.

Dave demanded excellence and people gave it. He demanded hard work and people gave it. He demanded loyalty and *he* gave it.

In 2013, David T. Traitel was the recipient of the Uncommon Commitment Award, an honor given to individuals making outstanding contributions to the Hoover Institution. To further demonstrate the Traitels' commitment to the Hoover Institution, a wing named after David and Joan Traitel was completed in 2017.

One team member from the sales department, the national military director, wrote this speech below for Dave Traitel's retirement ceremony. This simple speech has a very profound message: "First you are here, and then you're not." It is a memorable and honorable way to close the final chapter of Nutro's story.

> In his commencement speech last year at Whitman College, Eric Idle, the star of Monty Python said, "Life has a very simple plot: First you're here and then you're not." And so it seems to me that 17 years have gone by very quickly and with that, so many friends, past and present.
>
> For those of you with whom I have worked most closely, I want to say thank you for your friendship and support. . . . I want to say thank you for the opportunity you have given me to wake up every day with a sense of purpose and passion, and the chance to serve a cause greater than myself.
>
> And for those of us who will report to work tomorrow morning at zero-dark-thirty, I ask that you do so joyfully, because retirement will come to each of us in our turn. It is not something to be rushed or encouraged, because it too brings its own set of challenges.
>
> Therefore, I ask that you live each day mindfully and in appreciation of the gifts you have been given, for there are no guarantees of tomorrow, only today. So, when you leave here tonight, please remember this one thing: "Life has a very simple plot: First you're here, and then you're not."

The company changed ownership in May of 2007 and has since undergone eight reorganizations—or "revitalizations," as the new management called it—giving the phrase "first you're here and then you're not" more meaning than just simply retiring.

At the peak of Nutro's success, over 350 sales people worked at the company, most across six national regions, and a dozen members of the international team. When Mars purchased the company in 2009, Bob Gamgort, then-President of Mars, shared this about Nutro: "The sales team was the crown jewel. We bought the company to complete our portfolio and because of the sales team. We want to integrate Nutro into Mars and invigorate the passion the Nutro sales team has into Mars."

Beginning in 2009, with an economy in a recession and a reevaluation of the hierarchy, the new ownership decided to reorganize Nutro Products. Eight years have passed and eight reorganizations have taken place. When we look around in the pet industry today, we notice that many of the people who work in it started with Nutro products. Make no mistake; if you are "*legacy Nutro,*" you are still the "*crown jewels.*" No matter where you are and where you go, we will always be a *band of brothers!*

Author's Note

Fact or Fable?

"A people without the knowledge of their past history, origin and culture is like a tree without roots."
—Marcus Garvey

Historians consider what they do to be a real craft. They are not just excellent storytellers; they seek the truth by conducting impartial research. Once they introduce a new fact, most historians will record the information so future generations can learn from it.

While history is the study of the past, it also helps to provide an identity for people or organizations. Of course, an identity sometimes becomes muddled over time, and it's up to current generations to seek out the facts to create a new and more accurate account of the actual events.

As authors, we discovered both unrecorded and new facts when doing research for this book that differ from the original stories we and many others had heard about Nutro. As such, the lineage of this documented story has three family trees to review.

FABLE

According to company folklore, there are a few stories about how the company got started. One story is how John Saleen purchased the company (Figure 25) in 1926 from a British entrepreneur, James Spratt. As the story goes, Saleen then sold the company to David Traitel.

FIGURE 25: THE NUTRO COMPANY PRODUCT BROCHURE

Another published story is from the *Nutro Products Professional Development Booklet* (1996), a manual given to all sales representatives and demonstrators that the company hired. This booklet references the company's history in the following way: "Branded packaged pet food is an English innovation dating to the late 1800s . . . an English family named Spratt was manufacturing dog food in the U.S. In 1926 they sold their equipment to a gentleman named John Saleen . . . [who] relocated to Los Angeles and formed Nutro Products, Inc."

We uncovered further evidence via a video created by two company marketing gurus in 1989, which elaborates: "In 1895, Mr. Spratt brings his company to New York and later in the 1920s he built a second plant in San Francisco. Mr. Spratt decides he wants to go back to England and sells the rights to his dog food formula to John Saleen in 1926. John Saleen then becomes the founder of Nutro Dog Food Company."

This is where we want to address some facts—specifically, to note that James Spratt died circa 1880 and sold his company in 1878 to three gentlemen. Additionally, John Saleen was born in 1918 and passed away in 2002. This means that it is *impossible for James Spratt and John Saleen's paths to have crossed.* This fable was more of a romanticized tale and probably just a cleaner story that the Nutro marketing department may have conjured up.

So what *really* happened, then?

Herben Serois Lineage

The first family tree is Herben Serois, a name most people in the pet industry have not heard. On September 1, 1931, Herben Serois started a small pet food company that he named the Nutro Dog Food Company. Contrary to the previously told romanticized story, *Herben* was the founder, not John Saleen, and certainly not James Spratt.

Herben's business was located in the heart of Santa Monica, California. The Nutro trademark, approved in 1936, was to encompass dog food, cat food, and fox food. Herben ran his company until his death at the age of 63 in 1942. Little is recorded on Herben that we could find. Only his obituary, his grave marker (Forest Lawn Memorial in Glendale, California), the United States Patent Trade Mark filing (see Figure 26) and a few other historical facts previously mentioned in chapter 4.

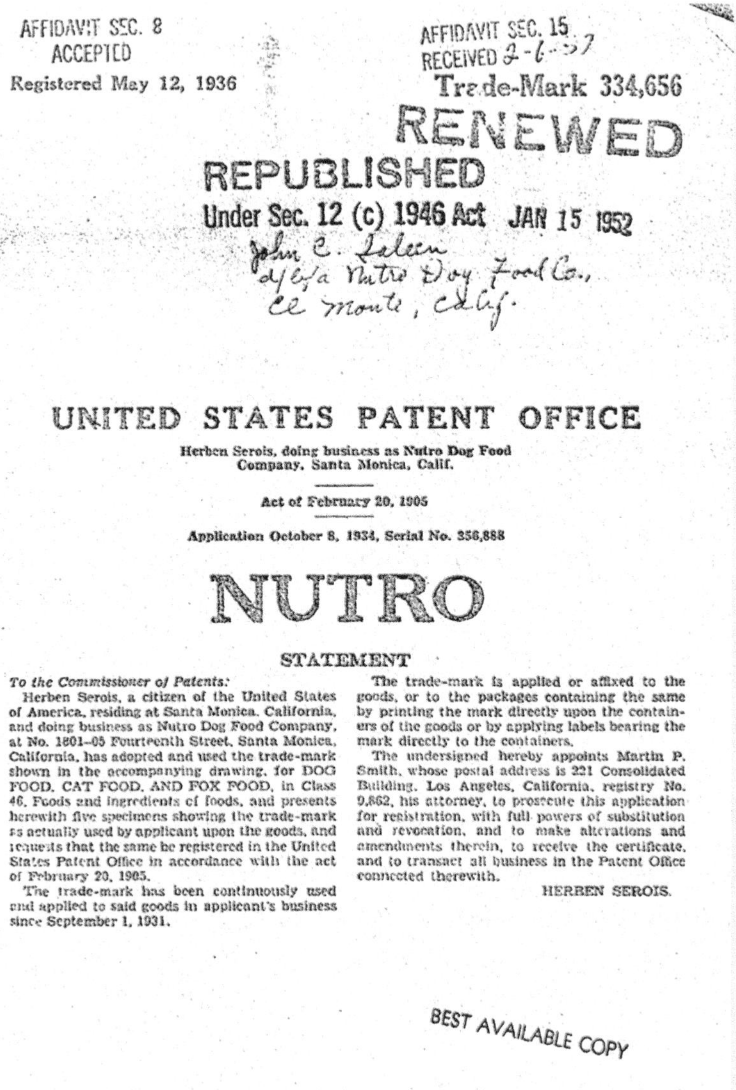

AFFIDAVIT SEC. 8
ACCEPTED

Registered May 12, 1936

AFFIDAVIT SEC. 15
RECEIVED 2-6-57

Trade-Mark 334,656

RENEWED

REPUBLISHED
Under Sec. 12 (c) 1946 Act JAN 15 1952
John C. Saleen
d/b/a Nutro Dog Food Co.,
El Monte, Calif.

UNITED STATES PATENT OFFICE

Herben Serois, doing business as Nutro Dog Food Company, Santa Monica, Calif.

Act of February 20, 1905

Application October 8, 1934, Serial No. 356,888

NUTRO

STATEMENT

To the Commissioner of Patents:

Herben Serois, a citizen of the United States of America, residing at Santa Monica, California, and doing business as Nutro Dog Food Company, at No. 1801-05 Fourteenth Street, Santa Monica, California, has adopted and used the trade-mark shown in the accompanying drawing, for DOG FOOD, CAT FOOD, AND FOX FOOD, in Class 46, Foods and ingredients of foods, and presents herewith five specimens showing the trade-mark as actually used by applicant upon the goods, and requests that the same be registered in the United States Patent Office in accordance with the act of February 20, 1905.

The trade-mark has been continuously used and applied to said goods in applicant's business since September 1, 1931.

The trade-mark is applied or affixed to the goods, or to the packages containing the same by printing the mark directly upon the containers of the goods or by applying labels bearing the mark directly to the containers.

The undersigned hereby appoints Martin P. Smith, whose postal address is 221 Consolidated Building, Los Angeles, California, registry No. 9,862, his attorney, to prosecute this application for registration, with full powers of substitution and revocation, and to make alterations and amendments therein, to receive the certificate, and to transact all business in the Patent Office connected therewith.

HERBEN SEROIS.

BEST AVAILABLE COPY

FIGURE 26: NUTRO TRADEMARK APPLICATION FROM THE USPTO

Saleen Lineage

John Saleen (born in 1918) became the new owner of Nutro Dog Foods in approximately 1947. For the next two decades, John and his family operated the business locally in El Monte, California. But as discussed in chapter 4, John's children did not have the same passion for running the family business as he did. Each of John's children began their careers, and John later agreed to sell his operation to Ed Brown, David Traitel, and a few other silent partners.

Over time, David Traitel bought out his partners and became the sole owner for many years. Eventually, Dave found himself in a similar position to John Saleen: his children did not want to run the family business. Finally, in 2006, Bain and Associates solidified a management-led buyout deal in obtaining Nutro Products for just a smidge over $1 billion. Just a few short years later, the company was set up to be acquired by Mars, Incorporated, and was purchased for $2.1 billion. Not a bad investment!

James Spratt Lineage

Most people would agree that James Spratt is the founding father of the creation of commercial dog food. But little is known about Spratt, and gaining historical information on this elusive man has been challenging. We know that he was born in Ohio and relocated to the United Kingdom around 1850 for varying reasons. James invented many items, and had patents for electrical lightening conductors, which is what most authors publish about him, as well as for Hermetic Sealing, Improvements in Food for Cattle, and of course his legendary Fibrine Meat Dog Cakes. The last item is what has given Spratt his notoriety in the pet food industry.

Spratt formed his company in 1860 and as described in chapter 2, just a few years before his death (circa 1880), he sold it to Edward Wylam. In 1885, Edward Wylam added two partners, C.J. Wylam and Beetham Batcheor, and the three partners invested a combined 200,000 British pounds. Soon thereafter, the company went public under the name Spratt's Patent Limited. After being incorporated, the operation moved to New York in 1895 with other offices in Newark, New Jersey.

After Spratt's death, his company's lineage continued in England and the United States, where it also gained new distribution. In 1950, General Mills purchased Spratt's Patent Limited; in 1961, Spiller's acquired the company and initiated a few name changes. In 1968 they called it Spratt's Patent Holdings, then changed it again in 1972 to Spillers Food Limited. Nestle then acquired Spillers for 715 million British pounds. Finally, in 2004 Spratt's Patent Limited patent is finally laid to rest and dissolved.

As authors and quasi-historians, we share these three family trees to reveal the actual accounting of ownership and a historical timeline. The story muddled over time is the ownership of Nutro. The story of the company's beginning that has been told over time goes like this:

1. Nutro began in 1926.
2. John Saleen bought the company from James Spratt, a British entrepreneur.
3. John later sold the company.

Contrary to popular belief, though, James Spratt never owned Nutro, never brought the company to the U.S. and never sold it to John Saleen. While the Spratt company did come to the U.S., James was not the one who made the transition. We must therefore give credit for Nutro's humble beginnings to Herben Serois, a name that, until now, had been virtually ignored in the history of pet food making.

Herben Serois applied for a trademark on October 8, 1934, which was later approved in 1936. He died in 1942, and his company was sold to the Saleen family. Herman ran the business along with his homemade meatloaf for dogs and foxes.

Mike Saleen recounted, "Sometime around 1947, my father purchased the Nutro Dog Food company from his uncle."

John owned the company until he sold it to Ed Brown and David Traitel in 1976. The company was later sold to Bain and Associates in a management-led acquisition.

It is currently owned by Mars, Incorporated, and has been since May 2007.

Appendix

The Nutro 10 Consumer Commandments

Author and source: Dewey Long

A wise man and visionary, Dave Traitel was tempted by the low-hanging fruit in the garden of feedin'. In the third month of our year 1985, Max was created. And it was good. Formulated for skin and coat and unlike those that came before, it was not born of bone or guts, but from meal gathered from the finest shepherds in the land: chicken, lamb, and rice.

The product differentiated from others by these ingredients had a story that needed to be told. Mr. Traitel summoned his disciple, Ladd Hardy, to load up the Max two by two into his station wagon and head to the promised land of Burbank, California.

People came from all around to see the product and hear the story, and they were converted. To further spread the word, comparative charts were placed throughout the land so that all may learn and benefit from their teachings.

Max was undeniably the best pet food in the world. The problem was how to get the message—the Nutro story—out to all the people. Should we follow our predecessors down the path of no-growth ruin via television, radio, magazines, and newspaper? These evil media formats, so detached from personal contact, were not the answer. Most pet food purchases result from recommendation. How, then, could we gain that recommendation?

Although all pet food peddlers say the same things about palatability, digestibility, skin and coat, and stool volume, no one can say their food outperforms Nutro. Better performance through better ingredients—*that* is the Nutro difference.

To tell this story and gain recommendation, we must go forth and multiply ourselves through other people. By building lasting relationships through trust, integrity, and accountability. How do we build that trust and that relationship? Think consumer.

Let's talk about the 10 Consumer Commandments that each Nutro pet food peddler must know:

1. Thou shalt know thy product and its benefits and why it is different.
2. Empathize with the customer. Help them understand how Nutro Products can solve their problems.
3. Be organized and efficient—time is precious.
4. Be prompt—quick response earns respect.
5. Follow through; build loyalty.
6. Provide solutions. Anyone can define a problem. Successful people provide solutions.
7. Be on time. Don't miss your opportunity.
8. Work hard. Keep your customers satisfied.
9. Be enthusiastic. It is contagious.
10. Be honest.

Acknowledgments

Billion Dollar Kibble was inspired by all those who, as we often said at Nutro Products, took the road less traveled. Everyone at Nutro used this saying to refer to the strategy that we did not use and instead favored the one that certainly took more fortitude.

Without the dedication of every individual who worked for and with Nutro, none of this would be possible. We pay special remembrance to James Spratt, whom numerous authors have recognized as someone who saw a niche and made a pet food that would revolutionize the way people would feed their dogs forever.

A special heartfelt acknowledgment goes out to Steve Saleen, whose drive and passion has impacted two industries: pets and cars. Steve's insights were invaluable in giving shape to the true beginnings of our book. Since the passing of his father, John, he was able to share memorabilia and stories with us.

Another name that must be recorded in the history books of pet food and has not until now is Herben Serois. Back in 1931, Herben was the original founder of the Nutro Dog Company. Little is known or written on Herben, and it has been painstaking, yet incredibly rewarding, to dig up the information that we have on this entrepreneur.

Finally, were it not for Dave Traitel and Ed Brown taking a leap of faith and buying the company, none of us would have the extended family that we do today.

Inspired by a poem written by Robert Frost, Nutro Products used the motto "the road less traveled" to motivate a sales team to realize that "selling one bag of a food at a time" would lead to success in the retail industry. Most importantly, the company changed the lives of pets and influenced the way pet parents would purchase their dog and cat food.

Two roads diverged in a yellow wood,
And sorry I could not travel both
And be one traveler, long I stood
And looked down one as far as I could
To where it bent in the undergrowth;

Then took the other, as just as fair,
And having perhaps the better claim,
Because it was grassy and wanted wear;
Though as for that the passing there
Had worn them really about the same,

And both that morning equally lay
In leaves no step had trodden black.
Oh, I kept the first for another day!
Yet knowing how way leads on to way,
I doubted if I should ever come back.

I shall be telling this with a sigh
Somewhere ages and ages hence:
Two roads diverged in a wood, and I—
I took the one less traveled by,
And that has made all the difference.

~Robert Frost

Those who took the road less traveled . . .

In memory of:

Andrea Raich
Bill Sandifer
Bubba Green
Chuck Davis
Dan Grampp
Dan Provenzano
Dave Traitel Jr.
Debbie Markson
Don Taffy
Frank Hon
George Buttes
Haig Kanosian
Herben Serois
Howard Hood
Jack Hahn
Jason Forward
Jeff Petersen
John Saleen
Larry Abramovitz
Linda Adolph
Kenny Owen
Scott Huntley: BT West

Still in our midst:

Aaron Schmidt
Adrian Hernandez
Adriana Valencia
Agustin Romero
Akruti Pathak
Al Cline
Al Treccia
Alan Colna
Alejo Valez
Alex Solis
Alfredo Sotelo
Alicia Cac
Alissa Sablan
Allen Arias
Alma Avena
Alvaro Manzo
Andrew Budrow
Andrew Hogan
Andy Crawford
Andy Crowell
Andy Epping
Andy Faessler
Angela Regan
Angela Weir
Anita Revelles
Anthony Giudice
Anthony Quinn
April Palacious
Ariel Angeles
Art Munoz
Arthur Peyser
Arturo Mejia
Austin Newton
Bac Nguyen
Barry Curtis
Becky Soto
Beth DeLeon
Beth Emhoff
Bill Barry
Bill Fitts
Bill Green
Bill McElhaney
Bill Morat
Bill Rahn
Bill Sandifer
Bob VanColt
Brad Cochrane
Brad Plein
Brandi Gerhardt
Brandon Due
Brenda DuBois

Brenda Neidlinger
Brent Humphrey
Brett Davis
Brian Avants
Brian Bogart
Brian Cunningham
Brian Gay
Brian Records
Brian Smith
Bruce Voss
Bryan Allen
Buddy Rehkopf
Cameron Houser
Cameron Passey
Carl Mokosak
Carlos Contreras
Carlos Diaz
Carlos Rivera
Carmel Vargas
Carol Linkins
Carol Strode
Cesar Mendoza
Chad Calhoun
Chad Cooper
Chad Maddox
Chad Polski
Charles Keating
Chris Dempsey
Chris Dennis
Chris Kenady
Chris Smith
Chris Wilburn
Christelle VanSteenkiste
Christian Hoehn
Christian Nourry
Christie Cooper
Christina Juarez
Christine Carrion
Christopher Dempsey
Chuck Lata
Cinda LaBaron
Cindy Johnson
Cindy Vasquez
Claudia Estevez
Clayton Mariotti
Clifton Foster
Colin Lundrigan
Conny Versendaal
Corinne Blair
Corey Lanier
Cory Parsons
Craig Lammers
Craig Saling
Damian Cooper
Dan Calkins
Dan Fortuna
Darcy Hagen
Daren Blais
Daren Simmons
Darlene Kurtzweil
Dave Horton
Dave Kelly
Dave King
Dave Kravis
Dave Martin
Dave McDonald
Dave Orr
Dave Otting
Dave Weigel
Davia Frias
David Ivester
David Nye
David Silver
Deb Wilson
Debbie Evans
Debbie Stampley
Debby Davis
Deby Lu
Denise Montenagro
Denise Vega
Dennis Pollard
Dennis Sullivan
Dennis Warnke
Dennoy Ly
Dewey Armstrong

Dewey Long
Diana Romero
Dirk Litten
Don Carlson
Don Hoang
Don Law
Don Pabisz
Don Williams
Donald DeLaCerna
Donald Young
Donnell Sablan
Doug Amdur
Doug Sterling
Douglas Fischer
Earl Smith
Edvin Tiguila
Edward Mittwer
Eli Ellis
Elisas Cornejo
Elizabeth Ramirez
Emilio Rivera
Enrique Santamaria-Rivera
Eric Dwyer
Eric Partenheimer
Erica Flores
Erin Lee
Erin Patterson
Errol Brown
Esaul Orozco
Evelyn Mendoza
F. Malekzadeh
Fabrizio Spena
Faustino Baena
Felipe Castillo
Felix Hernandez
Fernando Del Campo
Flavio Ortiz
Francesca Waldron
Francisco Granados
Francisco Herran
Frank Frias
Frank MacMillan
Fred Corbett
Fred Kroeplin
Fred Smith
Fredy Gomez
Fritz Condon
Gail Riffel
Gary Crosslin
Gary Lentz
George Briscoe
George Iqueda
Gera Herrera-Sepulveda
Gerald Toussaint
Gerardo Hernandez
Gerard Kearns
Gerry Leukam-Ibberson
Gino Diaz
Gordon Ross
Greg Acari
Greg Braithwaite
Greg Hayden
Greg Hutsell
Greg Mandel
Greg McElhaney
Gregorio Espinoza
Gus Baltabois
Gustavo Renteria
Hannon Namahoe
Hans Sleeger
Hardy Frink
Harold Gillard
Haydee Woody
Hazel Paguio
Heather Gillespie
Heather Huertas
Hector Hernandez
Hector Martinez
Helen Sherry
Helena Keck
Ines Feijoo
Inga Rodriquez
Isabel Martinez

J. Change
J. Tomey
J.R. Winkler
Jack Hahn
Jack Murray
Jack Zubritzky
Jackie Bulger
Jackson Dering
Jade Dominique
James Kilton
James McClernon
James Simplot
James Talley
James Verdon
Janie Klatt
Jasmine Atar
Jason Bailey
Jason Cohen
Jason Desilva
Jason McCullagh
Jason McGull
Jason Montgomery
Jan Thydean
Javier Pulido
Jeanine McDonald
Jeff Barton
Jeff Hicks
Jeff King
Jeff Lysak
Jeff Mount
Jeff Nashar
Jeff Phillips
Jeff Postma
Jeff Rachu
Jeffrey Williams
Jel Cardoza
Jennifer Ketola
Jennifer Moffitt
Jeremiah Cooper
Jeri Gagne
Jerry Beaudion
Jerry Gagne
Jerry Harding
Jerry McDaniel
Jerry Serrano
Jerry Sicherman
Jerry Villanueva
Jerry West
Jerry Young
Jessica Sanchez
Jessie Oakley Slaton
Jesus Torres
Jill Blaylock
Jill Hunt
Jim Belser
Jim Gorrell
Jim Kepler
Jim Nerihs
Jim Simplot
Jim Wheeler
Jimmy Misiuk
Jo Hollingsworth
Joan Dillon
JoAnn Collins
Joaquin Munoz
Joe LoCicero
Joe Siciliano
Joel Cleveland
Joel Dillard
Joey Rogers
John Bennett
John Cariglio
John Eishenheimer
John Henderson
John Hooks
John Luisi
John Martin
John Rivera
John Ruter
John Senich
John Vanaken
Jorge Ramirez
Jose Colunga
Jose Esparza
Jose Noelmestas
Jose Segura
Joyce Verham

Juan Puentes
Juan Ramirez
Juan Villegas
Kate Sterling
Kathryn Ricks
Kathy Garrison
Kathy Lambert
Kayleen Taylor
Keith Elrod
Keith Sweet
Kelly Burns
Kelly Donohue
Kelly Wucherpfennig
Ken Bush
Ken Nowak
Ken Purchase
Ken Wiechman
Kendle Newson
Kevin Hunt
Kevin Keller
Kim Douglass
Kim Goldberg
Kim Mailloux
Kim Mann
Kim Mitchell
Kim Scott
Kimberly Foutz
Kip: BT West
Kirk Impecoven
Kirk Olischefski
Kirk McClaren
Kristy Murphy
Kui Kawata
Kurt Gergle
L. Akinyemi
L. Miranda
Ladd Hardy
Lance Watkins
Lanny Bartlett
Larry Abramovitz
Larry Glick
Larry Martinez
Larry Waranka
Laura Johnson
Laurie Hagelis
Leigh Garry
Lenore Bartlett
Leo Pinal
Leslie Bell
Leticia Gallegos
Lewis Whelchel
Lia Rivadeneyra
Lilia Garza
Lisa Cromwell
Lisa Lamrakis
Lisa Laughlin
Lisa Miller
Lisa Pierce
Lisa Steltemeier
Lizbeth Sanchez
Lori Johnson
Lori Joyce
Lori Wojack-Thomas
Louis Mouton
Luca Bianchini
Lucas Bosco
Ludy Frew
Luis Gonzalez
Luis Raya
Luis Santillan
Lyle Starr
Lynn Driscoll
Lysa Richards
Manuel Almaguer
Marcelino Solis
Marcella Perez
Marco Ramirez
Margaret Goodall
Margie Moss
Maria Barbosa
Maria Castro
Maria Sanchez
Marie Kinder
Marina Murillo Sanchez

Marina Scholefield
Mario Lomeli
Mark Anderson
Mark LaCorte
Mark Larson
Mark Mount
Mark Paepke
Mark Reed
Mark Sorge
Mark Wareing
Martha Garcia
Martha Puente
Martin Garcia
Martin Young
Martyn Bee
Mary Hooks
Maryline River
Mat Pira
Matt Chisolm
Matt DeFreitas
Matt Dixon
Matt Kimmel
Matt Thomas
Matthew Lorfing
Megan Carbonne
Melissa Colpitts
Melissa Done
Meredith Taggert
Mia Lugo
Michael Amador
Michael Ferraro
Michael Gagne
Michael Green
Michael Justice
Michael Manjarrez
Michael Rivard
Michael Romero
Michael Rosick
Michael Scott
Michael Usery
Michelle Dickerson
Miguel Gutierrez
Mike Bioini
Mike Carr
Mike Chandler
Mike Gagne
Mike Green
Mike Hale
Mike LeVan
Mike Munoz
Mike Poss
Mike Satterwhite
Mitch Finn
Moises Negrete
Mynor Peralta
Myrna Lamera
Nancy Cantwell
Nancy Carr
Nancy Heiss
Neil Borne
Odette Coco
Odette Kirby
Olber Tadeo
Onyango Edwards
Ora Rittiket
Oscar Miranda
P. Weisbery
Pam Falcone
Patricia Koonter
Patricia Timmons
Patrick Hamill
Patrick Murphy
Patti Boehm
Paul Hoeft
Paul Leaming
Paul Pierson
Paul Sopsic
Paul-Eric Boulanger
Pedro Gonzalez
Pedro Gonzalez
Peggy Pleins
Peggy Pennington
Pepito Canonizado
Pete Shepherd
Peter Trevino
Pierre Gadbois
RaChelle Baca

Rafael Magallon
Rafi Kalachian
Ralf Klingebiel
Ralph Pena
Ramiro Sanchez
Ramon Napoles
Ramona Ramire
Randy Hubbard
Raquel Hernandez
Ray Navarro
Raymond Zumfelde
Rebecca Mekee
Renee Ganey
Reyes Garcia
Ricardo De La Cruz
Rich Zanetti
Richard Ueltxchi
Rick Celentano
Rick Petts
Rik Clark
Rob Glenn
Rob Johnson
Rob Lawson
Rob McCarthy
Robaab Amjadi
Robert Beatty
Robert Esquivel Sr.
Robert Glenn
Robert Hutter
Robert Lawson
Robert Nailon
Robert Rabichuk
Robert Vanas
Robert Young
Roberto Ruiz
Robin Florio
Rogelio Rabaan
Roger Clark
Roger Hyde
Roland Caramagna
Romy Francisco
Ron Ong
Ron Sanderson
Ronald Vinhateiro
Rosa Maneri
Rosalie Garcia
Ruben Felix
Rudy Leschke
Russ Lowell
Rusty Worstell
Ruth Kennedy
Salvador Ramos
Sam Shum
Samuel Galdamez
Sandra Perez
Sandy Hayes
Sandy Kasten
Saul Acosta
Scott Abrams
Scott Haff
Scott Keller
Scott Reinhardt
Scott Springfield
Scott Warwick
Sean Heisler
Sergio Barios
Sergio Milia
Shane Allgood
Shane Giardino
Shane Niles
Shannon Seiler
Sharie Fontana
Sharon Machlik
Sharon Morton
Shawn Owen
Shawnda Navarro
Skip Kroeger
Stacey Hudson
Stan Goodman
Stan Grumbeck
Stanford Gilbert
Stephen Lindsay
Stephen Tait
Steve Buccelli
Steve Buzzi
Steve Callahan
Steve Chan

Steve Hallford
Steve Nelson
Steve Reed
Stu Ray
Sue Wei
Sue Yolman
Susan Lutz
Susan Torres
Susan West
T. Coombes
Tamara Cerven
Taryn Herder
Ted Walker
Teresa Hill
Terry Halteman
Terry Manheim
Terry Thomann
Theresa Johnson
Thomas Flayhan
Tiffany Tuck
Tim Gallagher
Tim McMahon
Timothy Scoullar
Timothy Treadwell
Tineke Timmermans
Tom Howell
Todd Hyatt
Tom Cameron
Tom Caramanica
Tom Kapocious
Tom Latoza
Tom Serizawa
Tomas Rivas
Tony Miller
Tracy Hall
Tracy Morrison
Trevor Snelling
Troy Firth
Troy LaBranche
Troy Lebo
Tynna McChesney
Valerie Buford
Valerie Ybarra
Veronica Rumishek
Vicki Hargis
Vickie Akau
Victoria Chavez
Virginia Diaz
Ward Reynolds
Warren Montgomery
Wayne Bernal
Wayne Renfrew
Wayne Siegrist
Wes Boots
Wes Wagner
Whitney Piatkowsky
Woody Austin
Xavier Muratella
Yari Romandia
Yolande Hill
Yuki Morisawa
Zeferina Vidrio

About the Authors

Christie Cooper is the current President of Cooper Consulting Group. Previously she worked at the Nutro Company for 18 years in a variety of roles, including Regional Manager of National Accounts and Independent Territory Manager, as well as working in the training department for seven years alongside the Director of Training. While conducting training at Nutro, she found her true passion, which contributed to her vision: "*Inspire learning and leadership development to help leaders and teams be their best.*"

Christie has her doctorate degree in global leadership and change from Pepperdine University. Christie has been married to Howard for over 40 years and together they have a daughter, Lauren, who works in the pet food industry. Christie maintains her competitive spirit by showing and competing in dressage at the FEI (Fédération Équestre Internationale) levels.

Mary Hooks was employed with Nutro for her entire adult career. She started out as a Demonstrator, working short shifts with key retailers. She had many other roles that contributed to the significant growth at Nutro. She left the business in 2016 and currently enjoys her free time with her two grown girls, Meagan and Ashley, and her granddaughter, Ellie. Mary was born in Encino, California, on May 26, and has three brothers—Ed, David and Gavin—and a sister, Pam. Currently, she resides in Coeur d' Alene, Idaho, with her husband, Steve, of 34 years, and their golden doodle, Chuy.

Mary enjoys the adventure of life. She wakes up every day thankful for each new beautiful day with her friends and family. Mary struggled with dyslexia during high school and now serves as a role model to others by overcoming this challenge and having a successful career at Nutro.

Made in the USA
Monee, IL
13 March 2026

45463651R00085